How Cities Can Transform Democracy

How Cities Can Transform Democracy

Ross Beveridge &
Philippe Koch

polity

First published in 2023 by Polity Press

Polity Press
65 Bridge Street
Cambridge CB2 1UR, UK

Polity Press
111 River Street
Hoboken, NJ 07030, USA

ISBN-13: 978-1-5095-4598-8
ISBN-13: 978-1-5095-4599-5(pb)

A catalogue record for this book is available from the British Library.

Library of Congress Control Number: 2022935236

Typeset in 11 on 13 pt Sabon LT Pro
by Cheshire Typesetting Ltd, Cuddington, Cheshire, and
Printed and bound in Great Britain by CPI Group (UK) Ltd, Croydon

For further information on Polity, visit our website:
politybooks.com

Contents

Acknowledgements

This book project began in earnest in 2019 with the submission of a proposal to Polity Press. Since then, our editor Jonathan Skerrett has been very supportive and very good at asking the right questions at the right times. We thank him, the wider editorial team and the anonymous reviewers. We are also very grateful to Allan Cochrane and Roger Keil for their insightful and encouraging comments on earlier draft versions. Like any co-authored book this project involved a seemingly endless stream of conversations. Because of the pandemic and the distance between our homes, these generally took place on Zoom, with occasional meetings in Berlin, Glasgow, Kassel and Zurich. Workshops on urban austerity politics in Glasgow benefited from generous funding from the University of Glasgow and the Independent Social Research Foundation (ISRF). These were very enjoyable occasions, and we are grateful to all participants, especially co-organizer David Featherstone.

Ross thanks the Urban Studies Foundation, who financed his Senior Research Fellowship. He is also grateful for the welcoming environment in Urban Studies at the University of Glasgow and is very appreciative of the support offered during the tricky times of the pandemic. Further thanks go to Ludger Gailing and colleagues in Regional Planning at the Brandenburg University of Technology (BTU) as well as Timothy Moss and Matthias Naumann for all the related collaborations and conversations over the years. He is also indebted to staff at the Georg-Simmel Centre at the Humboldt University of Berlin, where he has enjoyed a visiting fellowship. Working with Markus Kip, as well as all the fantastic guests, on the Urban Political Podcast has been a very rewarding way of engaging with questions of urban democracy.

Philippe is very grateful to the Institute of Urban Landscape at the ZHAW Zurich University of Applied Sciences, which has offered great encouragement to pursue interdisciplinary work. In particular, he thanks Stefan Kurath, Regula Iseli, Andri Gerber, Simon Mühlebach and Andreas Jud. He has gained much inspiration from his activist networks, not least their ambiguous engagements with the state. His work on housing has profited from a collaborative research project funded by the Swiss Network of International Studies (SNIS) and led by Jennifer Duyne Barenstein. Finally, Philippe thanks his colleagues in urban publics Zurich, Hanna Hilbrandt, Lindsay Howe and David Kaufmann, for the creative discussions in the past and all those still to come.

We dedicate this book to Imogen and Carla, Hannah, Remy and Inez.

1

Why Cities?

The purpose of this book is to show that urbanites across the globe are transforming democracy as we know it. Scepticism may initially meet such a claim, a feeling that this is overstating the case. However visible and effective community organizers, housing activists and – some – public officials can be in cities, are they not marginal figures in the bigger picture of politics? Certainly, urban activists and politicians rarely dominate politics, either in numbers or impacts. However, in their actions we can often discern a different, distinctly urban way of doing democracy rooted in the principles of people working together for the common good. Seeing global politics on your doorstep, organizing with or against your neighbours, co-producing local services – many will understandably reply that, while all this seems very reasonable, is it not too far removed from, and insignificant to, the mainstream politics of national political parties, state institutions and media? Surely this is where we should look when we want to transform democracy, where real political power is at stake?

The book will contest this conventional view of politics. Indeed, it will turn it on its head to claim that democracy can never be stored up in formal institutions, assured and distributed by state power. National politics may indeed be the source of most formal political power, and in most places it provides the legal framework for representative democracy. However, it can never be the primary source of democratic power, that of the *demos*, the people, coming together in collective self-government. If we live, as many claim, in an urban world, then democracy belongs to those urbanites doing just this, finding common cause in the urbanity they produce. Democracy as understood here is a project of empowerment and equality, one that necessarily stands in opposition to, chafes against, subverts and is opportunistic towards, established forms of power, including state systems of democratic politics. Adopting such a view of democracy raises difficult questions as to how it can be extended and sustained in relation to existing political systems. The book attempts to address such concerns. It does not claim to have all the answers but it plots a way forward.

Cities play a crucial part in this. The 'urban' is not merely an incidental stage for democracy, but rather provides the conditions in which we propose a revival of the democratic imaginary of the 'city' as both a material and imagined place for the demos to come together. Urbanites in different locations across the planet are working collectively to reinvent the way we understand and practise self-government. Advancing global urbanization increasingly appears to be the frame within which such ideas and practices of democracy are developed. Urbanization is a world-making process, always simultaneously material, social and symbolic. It is best understood less as the process whereby archetypally urban forms of dense built environment expand (indeed, research shows that new urban form is very often *sub*urban) than as referring to the centrality of urban spaces and places to global systems of economy, culture and politics – the sense that the world now has an urban horizon. This might be seen in the extent to which certain big cities (London, New York, Tokyo) are crucial to the functioning of globally interlinked economies and societies, as nodes transmitting and receiving money, goods, services and even lifestyles, be they of the 'alpha' elite, the hipster and so on.[1] But the potency of the urban goes even further: it is the very grounds upon which the global economy is generated, where diverging interests take shape and compete for profit and prestige, justice and democracy.[2] The urban is where the local and global truly meet, as the housing crisis shows, with international real estate firms and the like capable of rapidly transforming housing and rental prices through investments in towns and cities of all sizes and strengths from Munich to Mülheim an der Ruhr.[3]

Urbanization alters places in uneven ways, generates new ones and shifts the meanings of existing ones. Prosperity and poverty can move from one place to another as globalized economic relations reshuffle themselves through urban form, expanding and shrinking urban places, giving rise to new *glocal* political and social constellations. Even though the forces of urbanization have been the subject of intense academic and public debates, the implications for democracy have yet to be fully considered. Against this background, this book tackles the question of the effects of urbanization on the possibilities for democracy.

The main argument being made here is that the diverse political practices and organizations found in urban spaces point to an alternative horizon of democracy, but one that can only be appreciated if we are prepared to relinquish conventional, increasingly dated understandings of the where, what and how of politics. Urbanization forces us not only to consider its potent real world implications. It also compels us to reconsider the way we look at politics and the vocabulary we use to think about democracy. A new and distinctly urban democratic project is already visible and real in many places – in housing struggles, in claims to citizenship, even in survival strategies – but has been overlooked by many scholars and politicians because of the dominance of state-centric understandings of democracy. Changing from what we term the 'state lens' on politics to the 'urban lens' helps to make sense of a wide range of practices, struggles and experiments that aim for self-government, articulate citizenship and interrogate the complicated relationship between urban society and the state. The notion of *the* 'city', so key to democratic theory, is crucial in many contemporary political projects not so much as a spatial entity but as a political idea and pledge about a place and the wider world. Urbanites struggle for the 'right to the city' by taking over urban space and reorganizing how it is produced, enjoyed and governed. Their claims to the 'city' may indeed encompass a place called a city (like Athens or Medellin) or may simply refer to a struggle for a stake within urban places, such as housing. Aims, strategies and practices are diverse, but the assumption that democracy is a spatial project is ever present. Taking inspiration from ongoing political projects, the book argues that now is the time to reimagine the city as a democratic idea, one that links a specific locale to collective practices and thereby contributes to this emergent urban democracy. Throughout the book, we will consider ideas or imaginaries of the city as important for past, present or future democratic projects. By using these terms, we foreground the city as a horizon of collective experience and imagination connecting political aspirations to material places in which people live and act.[4]

The reintroduction of the city in a world of nation states might appear a little obtuse. But the democracies of the nation states are currently in crisis, perhaps even retreat. At least since the global financial crisis of 2008/9 and the imposition of austerity in many countries worldwide, the legitimacy and efficacy of mainstream political parties – indeed of whole political systems – in mediating between the rights of citizens and the interests of business have been ever more contested. If, as some claim, the nation state experienced a revival during the Covid-19 pandemic, it was surely primarily one of crisis management rather than democratic legitimacy. After decades in which neoliberal rationality has reshaped politics in the mould of economics, the demos has been undone, to paraphrase the title of the political theorist Wendy Brown's book.[5] Democratic ideas of citizenship and equality have been degraded through their exposure to market ideas of consumerism and competition. The resulting disenchantment of democracy has seen the rise of far-right populism in the mainstream of those democracies usually keen to emphasize their stability and longevity, like the USA, the UK and the Netherlands.[6] Scholars such as Cornel West trace causal links between the failings of (neo)liberal democracy and the rise of a contemporary fascism associated with Donald Trump and others.[7] Such developments are occurring on the back of at least twenty years in which growing numbers of scholars and commentators have countered widespread complacency about the state of democracy, observing growing political disenchantment and depoliticization.[8] Shaping these processes is globalization and the growing strength of global corporations in the affairs of all nations, be they formally democratic or not. At present, it is legitimate to ask not what we can do to save nation-state democracies, but if there might be a more democratic way of doing politics.

But isn't the idea of the city as the realm of democracy an ancient one, entirely unsuited to an urbanizing world? That the city has a special relation with democracy does indeed go all the way back to the roots of political theory in ancient Greece. The small-scaled, bounded and exclusionary Athenian Republic is not, however, the source of inspiration for our arguments, at least not in the sense it is commonly referred to. The starting point has to be the often intense heterogeneity and global interdependence of urban societies. The 'city', understood as a distinct spatial form, social configuration or 'authentic arena of political life', to borrow Murray Bookchin's term,[9] offers us little hope in a context in which cities are blurring into variegated urban-social forms, suburbanized, regionalized, even 'rurbanized'. Instead, the point of departure must be the process driving the spatial, economic and political transformations of contemporary societies – urbanization – and the purpose is to resituate democracy in this encompassing process.

In this project, the city is nevertheless instrumental. Not, however, in the conventional sense where the city is synonymous with urban cores often with historical meaning and a distinct spatial and political form. The argument of the book is that the city is the imagined and actual place where people come together in their aim to access and govern their immediate socio-material environment.[10] By doing so, they change the way we can understand and practise democracy in the age of urbanization. This can happen in cities conventionally understood, like Amsterdam, Buenos Aires or Tel Aviv. But the city can also have no name, no clear institutional or spatial form, and yet still be apparent as a claim to democracy, an horizon of political practices. Against a pessimistic reading of our predicament – namely, that the democratic project collapses with the nation state, or that the nation state dismantles democracy to reclaim sovereignty – this book detects a more hopeful political future, one that reclaims the city in and against processes of urbanization.

Our arguments draw on global examples of contemporary political practices and collective acts which are distinctly *urban* in their attempts to expand democracy. They are urban as they are situated within, targeted towards, use and develop resources from urbanized spaces.[11] They can be read as aiming for an *urban* democracy in their pursuit of a project of urban collective life. To 'read' these practices, the book draws, necessarily, on multiple literatures within the field of urban studies, and brings them into dialogue with the radical democracy tradition in political thought. There is much ground to cover. The book is not a work of high theory nor deep empirical research, nor one offering falsifiable hypotheses and the like. It is, rather, an 'intervention': an attempt to shape political ideas, debates and practices. There is sustained engagement with the state of the art in urban studies, and more particularly with the implications of 'planetary urbanization' for how we imagine and practise the 'city' and 'democracy'. We find inspiration in radical traditions of democracy. Here institutions are less important than practices. An understanding of democracy in which the demos is forged through shared political experiences, and situated rather than given, runs through the book. Of course, frictions are present at times, but the spirit is one of an 'engaged pluralism',[12] aiming to advance not a single school of thought or discipline, but ideas and arguments on the urban conditions of politics and democracy. The rest of this chapter provides the basis for the arguments that follow by sketching the relations between democracy, the city and urbanization, before briefly outlining the chapters to come.

What is left of the city after urbanization?

Scholarly discussion on the relation between the city and democracy has witnessed something of a renaissance in recent years. Some scholars see the city as the great hope of democracy because cities, rather than nations, are best placed to organize politics in a context of deepening globalization and advancing urbanization. In this view, the city(-state) should be sovereign because cities are more cooperative, pragmatic and innovative than nation states, which are, in contrast, captured by ideological, competitive politics and the anachronistic dreams of nationhood.[13] Such optimism is, however, countered by those writers who direct our attention to the manifold ways in which cities have become more unequal and elitist, driven by a post-democratic consensus founded on neoliberal principles and practices.[14] To complicate matters further, there is a third position in the debate, which states that it is pointless even to think about the city, whether in hopeful or regretful terms, because – in a context of fragmentary global urbanization, which is generating (sub)urbanized regions and hollowing out cities – the city is a spatial and social form that no longer exists.[15] In this view, rather than being an agent of political change, the city haunts politics like a ghost of an urbanity past. And whatever urbanization has left of the city has often been turned into sites of speculative capitalism, extraction and dispossession. Many city centres are dominated by global chain stores and apartment blocks that lie empty because they are investments not homes; suburbs sprawl with rich enclaves nestled amongst densely populated slums and low income areas, carved up by road and rail infrastructures. These bitty remains do not seem the best places to look for democratic renewal. All in all, this begs the question: what, then, is the democratic potential of the city in times of urbanization?[16]

Urbanization not only transforms the physical surface of the globe, it also undermines the dominant conception of politics and democracy constructed around the nation and the sovereignty of the state and its bureaucratic institutions. Urbanization, as other scholars have argued, contributes to an informalization and de-centring of the state.[17] It destabilizes many boundaries on which nation states depend, inducing different densities and proximate diversities in various ways all over the world. To be sure, urbanization is by no means a uniform process homogenizing the globe. It is, fundamentally, a process by which the form and meaning of land, its various uses and the social relations around it, get transformed. What is more, the process of urbanization is often violent and rooted in longstanding practices of accumulation by dispossession. From the US subprime mortgage crisis and housing repossessions that triggered the global financial crisis, through broader processes of gentrification and displacement, urban renewal and forcible removal, to the financialization of housing and the crisis of rising rents, urbanization can be a brutal, profit-seeking process, loyal only to the so-called rules of the market and those who benefit most from them.[18] To say that the politics of the nation state is partly undermined by this process does not imply, however, that the power of the state is not vital to spur urbanization in the first place. And yet, the effects of urbanization on the authority and steering capacity of state institutions are often detrimental. This is not per se emancipatory or liberating for urbanites.[19] Often market forces are unleashed in ever more destructive ways in the shadow or absence of the state. We are well aware of this reality: this dark side of urbanization runs through the book. Nonetheless, the effects of urbanization on state politics are also generative of democratic possibilities. We are thus mainly interested in how urbanization can (re-)awaken alternative modes of collective organization and self-rule. Some of them are still nascent, others are already flourishing across the globe, albeit often in a fragmented way, based on distinct histories and ambitions.

What the city's role is in furthering or even transforming democracy in the age of urbanization is a question with no easy answer. As said, in morphological terms, the city has lost its shape and boundaries. Where the city begins and the hinterland starts is no longer obvious – if it ever really was. The city seeps into the countryside as infrastructure networks extend and intensify, as housing and commerce edge outwards and urban cultures and economies circulate, with lifestyles, tourism and goods moving and blurring the distinctions between urban and rural. Glimpses of what might be associated with the 'countryside' often pop up in the city as urban nature and even wilderness.[20] The expansion of the built environment, economic relations and interdependencies across cities and states and across the urban/rural divide undermines traditional notions of the city as a self-evident category or a distinct type of settlement, and problematizes 'the city lens' often implicitly used in scholarly work.[21] On what grounds, then, can it be argued that the city retains political and democratic purchase?

A way forward can be found in the 'southern turn' in urban studies, which offers a means of reimagining the idea of the city for current conditions. In these postcolonial debates, the city or the urban have never been self-evident or 'natural' categories of political analysis. Instead, Ananya Roy and other scholars engaging with urbanization in the global south are concerned with 'the processes through which the urban is made, lived and contested'.[22] What these perspectives share is an understanding of the city as always already intertwined with the politics of urbanization. The city is of interest as a 'category of practice' instead of a category of analysis.[23] Indeed, this body of literature forces us to think about how new theories and vocabularies of the urban might give way to more democratic modes of practice and engagement.[24]

The city, as with most 'everyday' concepts, has an undeniable affective and political power, albeit, or rather because, it distorts our view of things. The city as a political idea can not only generate objects of contestation but can also be used and channelled for space-shaping practices and to connect different struggles in and against urbanization.[25] As some scholars have argued, in terms of politics, urbanization levels the differences between centres, suburbs and urban peripheries.[26] Yet, the city as an actual place where material things, infrastructures and bodies come together, and at the same time where a distinct idea of commonwealth and collective purpose prevails, has democratic potential in the age of urbanization.

In the rest of the book we explore examples of the city as a democratic project from around the world. These include the coming together of social movements and city governments in the 'new municipalism' in places like Barcelona and Naples, which re-set relations between urban society and the state.[27] But inspiration is also drawn from housing struggles in different parts of the world which often strive for urban self-government. Throughout the book we discuss a multitude of practices, collectives and movements that are not always directly associated with conventional democratic politics at all. From stateless 'insurgent citizens' on the urban peripheries in the global south, through housing cooperatives and Critical Mass cyclist activists, to many others, we can detect an urban way of not just thinking about, but also doing democracy.[28] What we see in these practices is a common democratic impulse focused on the aim to self-govern urban spaces. Of course, these places and practices look different, have contrasting histories and embody different meanings; but they all claim and realize a right to the city, to be a part of, to enjoy and to co-determine their immediate environment. The city in this perspective is where citizens meet to deliberate and act in common, driven by a democratic ethos, no matter the spatial form of the place.[29] It is in this way that we think the city still has a part to play in the project of democracy, as a 'concrete utopia', already there in fragments, the project of politically creative beings embedded in urban collective life.[30]

Seeing democracy like a city

To see and appreciate the democratic potential of the city, however, we need to take *an urban view* of politics. By this we mean looking at politics not from the perspective of the nation state, but from the midst of things, within and through the spaces of the urban collective life, scanning the horizon of democracy shaped by urbanization.[31] Our arguments rest on the premise that we need to flip the common understanding of the relation between city and democracy. Cities are not merely the physical locations, political stages and sovereign institutions in the drama of democracy. If we want to draw on the historical relation between the city and democracy, we need to reflect on it in a different way. Urbanity shapes a different political life marked by proximate diversity, the deferral of sovereignty, and the complicated patterns of (self-)government situated in urban collective life.[32] Contemporary urbanization has moved the goalposts of democracy: as stated above, we cannot think of the city as a discrete form. However, urbanity can provide the conditions of democratic politics, and the city can provide the horizon of democracy.[33] The political practices we discuss here are attempts to realize this idea – they act upon the city as a political idea for democratization.

But what does this idea imply for our understanding of democratic politics more generally? We might think of democracy as being a political project concerned with the alignment of three constitutive elements. First and foremost, democracy is the rule of the people, the demos, to use the Greek term. But rule over what? Over their own lives? Yes, but it is more than that; it is about self-governing societies, finding common ground across difference, or what we call urban collective life. Achieving the rule of the people requires an engagement with the multiple forces shaping urban collective life – the struggle requires tools. This second element leads us to the third: the state, the dominant modern political actor, and for many the decider of the fate of democracy. In modern times, the project of democracy has been imagined largely in terms of the nation and representative democracy. The demos has become equated with the citizens of a nation, voters in elections; societies are after all national, and the state is organized along national lines. This has provided the conditions of democracy for the high modern period.[34] But if the grip of the nation and representative politics on democracy is slipping, then it must be possible, and may also be necessary, to reconfigure democracy.[35]

One way to reimagine democracy is to start from the assumption that it has no self-evident or privileged locus and is a process rather than a condition which can be institutionally shielded.[36] Practices of democracy might emerge everywhere. Parliaments, town halls, city squares are just some of the locations amongst many where democracy happens. Democracy can be articulated through a multitude of practices which do not necessarily comply with a distinct and enclosed form. Democratic meaning is not bound to a set of arrangements, like the nation state, or to any other formation for that matter. Consequently, this book does not offer a different model of democracy to be evaluated against others. Taking our cues from radical strands of democratic theory, we understand democracy as an open-ended project based on situated practices. The project of democracy is nurtured by an ethos of equality when it comes to defining shared troubles and the ways in which they should be addressed.[37] To detect a different imaginary of democracy, one which is aligned with urbanization, entails dropping the essentialist idea of a congruence of country (geography), people (society) and nation state (politics).

Democracy as rooted in the self-fashioning practices of the demos shifts us far away from abstract citizens, norms, values, preferences or (strategic) interactions and towards the material actions and tacit understandings of real people, citizens-in-action.[38] Hence, a shift from institutions to practices implies that we focus more on the (democratic) knowledge that is expressed in practices than on the sort of knowledge that institutions call their own and try to spread. For example, we are more interested in how neighbourhood collectives shape in a pressing fashion the urban spaces around them than in how established formal political actors design participatory planning processes. In this view of democracy, the physical space and the material transformations through which that space has been shaped become more important. This contrasts with most accounts of democracy, which do without the material environment in which democracy 'happens'. Further, for an urban democracy, place is more important than scale. Place is always multi-scalar, where the local and global merge.[39] Ultimately, if we avoid essentialist notions of country, nation and people then we can think differently of the collectives and political subjects that make up democracy.

This way of looking at the relation between the city as an idea and democracy as practice comes with a number of implications. First, 'cities' are not our empirical cases where we land in order to discover a new democratic model for the urban age. Rather, we are interested in democratic practices, places and publics situated in urban collective life and performing, as it were, the democratic vision of the city. The city is therefore a generative space of difference, akin to Henri Lefebvre's idea of 'differential space', a place where democratic urban society can come together, and as such the idea of the city has an imaginative and political force.[40]

Second, if the city as an idea and practice is also an alternative to the nation state, it is not a nation-state politics writ small. With the city comes an *urban* way of being political, one distinct from the state form. Over the course of the twentieth century – it seems – the idea and practice of democracy was bound closer to the institutional architecture, the collective identity and the capacity to act that the nation state promised. The urbanization-globalization nexus has, however, undermined the nation state in far-reaching ways. The current crises of democracy associated with nation states cannot be resolved by saving the nation state as a political locus and trying to recuperate it at the more flexible scale of the city.

Third, we see emergent political ideas and practices rooted within urbanization and aiming to democratize it. Urban collective life becomes the locus of democratic politics as collective claims arise in relation to the problems posed by urbanization itself. We identify a project of democratizing the urban: Who is entitled to be part of the urban? Who defines urban territories and projects?

And who gets the surplus value produced by urbanization itself? Hence, the urban democratic project is an attempt at being urban and becoming a political subject confronted by and confronting urbanization.

Democratic projects of the city

If the city is the democratic idea we want to advance in this book, what kind of politics can we expect? What inspiration can be drawn from the past and how must the present be navigated? In urbanized space, past visions of democracy are materialized and visible like sediments of long-gone experiments: in memorials to political leaders and struggles, in grand town halls, in vast social housing estates and in the spaces where infrastructures of water and sanitation emerge overground. Cities were often and still are places of democratic longing – as the German mediaeval phrase *Stadtluft macht frei*, 'city air makes you free', indicates. The city has offered in the past, and continues to offer today, resources, spaces of action and horizons of democracy. In the early 2000s, for example, cities across Latin America became subject to diverse and often transformative projects of popular sovereignty.[41] The new municipalism of the contemporary period, in Barcelona, Berlin and Amsterdam, actively engages with ideas of urban democracy.[42]

Yet, just as there is no single idealized urban form of the physical city, there is no single democratic vision of the city. As our reflections below show, changing patterns of urbanization and shifts in urban form are bound up with democratic visions and the political forces advancing them. Over the last 150 years, the urban – in particular how it is produced and who benefits and suffers within it – has become ever more central to political life, in a way that it was not earlier. It follows that the dream and fate of democracy is ever more entangled in the struggles over these processes of urbanization. And as the old political ambitions are sometimes still visible in the urban fabric, the visions of the present are interwoven with those of the past. The city and its democratic potentialities have a history to which current urban movements contribute and from which they also derive and depart.[43]

Arguably the most dominant perspective on the democratic potential of the city in political science and media commentary is that which ties its fate to that of the state. The outlines of this project have resonances with the classical city-state, even if the sovereignty of modern projects is encased within the sovereign system of nations and, increasingly, the global economy. Democracy here is aligned with the institutions of the state, legitimized through political representation. Once won, the state was to be used to transform urban space. The city in this project is a top-down political institution representing urban society. There is an identification of society and the public with the state. Forms of government are established which shape urban everyday life but remain at a distance from it. The goal is the democratization of housing, transport and other urban infrastructures and services. But 'democracy' is filtered through the state system. The highpoint for this project was the municipal socialist projects of the late nineteenth century and, particularly, the early twentieth.[44]

Municipal socialism

Municipal socialism has left lasting marks on the urban. Think of the iconic social housing projects of (Red) Vienna.[45] Less visibly, but just as embedded, are the ways of organizing, community symbols and places of struggles in many cities.[46] Municipalism has been understood as a diverse set of 'laboratories of decentralised economic life'.[47] Much of the governmental activity in the industrializing and urbanizing societies of the global north of this period was taking place at the municipal level. Alongside 'municipal enterprise' projects, where the state simply took ownership of a service but continued to pursue profit as before, 'municipal socialism' represented the first attempt to disrupt liberal logics of privatization and profit-making that prevented fair access to basic resources in the city.[48] The project of municipal socialism largely dried up as a general movement in the post-Second World War context of growing centralization and the emergence of a new state mode of production scaled to the national level. Before that, the local state, the municipality, became a project of democracy. In Weimar Berlin, the city's electricity, gas, water and sanitation utilities, along with its large public housing and transport programmes and parks, were important for many urbanities (and many since) 'not merely in providing basic services for a growing metropolis, but in making democracy real, both in terms of urban policies enabled and political aspirations contested'.[49]

The state was the locus of this democratic project, the provider of political resources and the democratizer of urban resources. Its reshaping of urban space in certain places should not be underestimated. It established socio-political spaces in which working-class people, previously excluded not only from formal politics but from the city itself, could access basic amenities and opportunities.[50] But even where municipal socialism was most successful, not all urbanites were included in this democratic project. Forces of capital may have been marginalized in many aspects of urban life, but they remained untouched more generally, continuing to drive urban economies. Furthermore, municipal socialism was mainly a project of the organized working class and social democratic parties aiming to represent what they perceived to be their interests. Municipal socialism was selective in terms of policies and organizational means. The marginalized position of the Siedler (Squatting) movement in the history of housing policy in Red Vienna is illustrative. In short, during the extreme housing crisis after the First World War, working-class families built their own homes at the edge of the city.

These unorganized and unregulated Brettldörfer were, however, a thorn in the side of the local state, who wanted control of housing. The social democratic government was quick in tying them to their own approach of cooperatives and other political associations, which linked them to the party and the state. The autonomy of the self-building movement – or the alternative in the alternative – was thus co-opted by state logics of municipal socialism.[51]

Contradictions were therefore at play in this project of democracy.[52] On the one hand, we can characterize it as a move to open up the resources of the city to a wider section of urban society, and to establish universal standards in the basics of urban everyday life.[53] It was an outcome of the growing strength of the labour, working-class and social democratic political parties. On the other hand, it was also a project of expanding local state power over urban space and its inhabitants. The horizon of democracy was framed by the state, its institutions and the rules and logics which shaped its functioning. Democracy existed only within the limits of this state-framed horizon.

Urban social movements

If the history of the state in modern urbanization offers highly ambivalent potential, its 'force', and main resource, is unequivocal: sovereignty. The rightful and ultimate use of violence and the capacity to make and remake law may rest on an oddly mythical centre, but they provide a clear political sphere as well as coordinates for a project of the city: win the state and transform the city with the power of the state.[54] In this sense, the local state becomes a locus for democratic projects intent on its sovereignty.

In the second half of the twentieth century, the city was the site and source for a different democratic struggle, one rooted in urban society, not the state. The city as a field of economic processes, cultural identities and social relations becomes productive in democratic terms because it creates a specific political subject, the urban social movement, which strives for urban democracy. As Castells argued, urban social movements of the 1970s and beyond were not political organizations that derived from class or other political associations. Rather, they were indicative of an ineluctably *urban* demos that took shape against the homogenization, bureaucratization and commodification of urban space.[55] The collective social power of cities had long been apparent in uprisings, riots and protests. However, the late 1960s and 1970s marked a transitional moment in urban politics and politics more generally. The student and workers' movements of 1968, the emergence of the New Left, and the urban social movements represented a shift in political thinking and acting. Rather than formal politics, the everyday was foregrounded as a plane of political action. Diverse collective forces mobilized against capitalism, but also against the state, seeking new forms of democracy based on participation and the empowerment of the marginalized and excluded: racial minorities, women, gay people, alternative communities, as well as the working class.[56]

These political projects became bound up with the emergence of the city as an idea of the 'globalized urban society – an unbounded metropolis – in the capitalist West'.[57] In the global north, the spatial transformation of cities themselves was reshaping political practices and democratic demands.[58] Urban issues like housing and transportation were foregrounded in struggles for justice and democracy, criss-crossing with movements resisting racism, homophobia, imperialism, colonialism, militarism, capitalism, consumption and patriarchy. Urban social movements in the 1970s sought to mobilize urban populations (rather than political parties) for different goals, such as changing policies, challenging urban planning processes and defending neighbourhoods.[59] They politicized everyday life. But their demands were generally articulated towards the state and they often sought democratization through state reform, especially in the form of increased political participation. Crucially, the urban also became a stake, something to be won back from the state and capitalist logics.

In this democratic vision of the city, the city is perceived and practised less as a political institution and more as a cultural and collective undertaking. Henri Lefebvre's idea of the city as 'oeuvre', and his claim for a 'right to the city', articulated in the wake of the 1968 movements, outlined a vision of the city as a collective project to be rescued from homogenization, commodification and bureaucratic rule. The right to the city is a claim to take part in and co-produce the city and to refuse to turn it into a tradeable and consumable product.[60] In this struggle, existing institutions and practices of the state are not the prime resources for democratic projects – indeed they often turn into enemies of the urban demos.

Reimagining the city in an urban age

It is against the backdrop of these democratic visions of the city that we outline our own contemporary idea of what the city might mean for democracy and how it might transform democracy in times of global urbanization. The projects of the city as 'democratic state' and as 'urban demos' continue to have political purchase and often inform contemporary struggles over the city. But they also point to a tension noted at the outset of this chapter: Urbanity and the state are generative of contradictions and frictions, which neither can effectively deal with. Urban society always exceeds the grip of the state.[61] Urbanization as a socio-material process retains an unpredictable and unruly character, even in contexts where authoritarian states seek to master it. Urban life provides its own possibilities, despite or even because of the attempts of those forces – state and market – blowing hard through it. The conditions of sociality and proximate diversity, of the world being in one urban place, are generative: socially of course, in terms of the conditions of everyday urban life, but also politically, in terms of the conditions of democracy.[62]

It is our contention that both politics and democracy are increasingly shaped by and orientated towards global urbanization as a set of driving socio-economic forces. By this we mean that urbanization reshapes the political conditions of our time and provides resources for democratic practices by producing places and objects of political contention, by spatializing politics through territories and communities, and by encompassing non-sovereign mundane ways of self-governance and everyday action.[63] Urbanization thus opens up distinctly urban ways of thinking about politics and democracy, where urban space and the city are not (just) the setting for democratic practices but rather the medium for them, having an effect on the form, meaning and practice of democracy.

As stated at the outset, the project of democracy that we set out here is not nostalgic about the city. Rather, it rests on gauging what urbanization has left of the city politically, in terms of democratic potential. The city is not simply a backdrop to politics, like the capital city setting for high political intrigue in and around parliament. Rather, the city is increasingly the stake of politics, a terrain on which exclusionary forms of economic and political rule can be expanded endlessly into everyday life – or resisted. Cities have become central to contrasting visions and practices of our future world. Our interest lies not in the Promethean and technocratic visions of the Smart City saving the world from climate change, but rather in those attempts to seek common cause and collective organization through the idea of the city.

This means also that we have to leave the city as a distinct physical form behind. As a spatial form it is confusing, unstable, difficult to know where it stops and starts. Gentrified, homogenized, hollowed-out centres, radical suburbs – the city's spatial markers simply cannot be relied upon.[64] Our search for democracy should not then lead us automatically to the centres, the town halls, the monumental squares the 'city' invokes. These city forms are often still intact, and have recently been productive, but their meanings have often been transformed beyond recognition. We should embrace the disconnection between topographical and democratic space. Actual spaces of democratic projects do not necessarily align with the maps and images we have of cities as democratic spaces. The city has democratic purchase exactly because its meaning is contested, evoked in a variety of ways and places, an outcome of urban collective life. Enmeshed with individual and collective hopes and fears, the city unfolds in contradictory and uneven processes.[65] This is, we claim, the contemporary democratic productivity of the city.

Outline of the book

Chapter 2 takes up the argument that political openings in global urbanization cannot be grasped if we cling to conventional models of politics centred on the state. In this chapter we consider the potential of seeing politics like a city. Looking across the rich debates on urban politics past and present, we argue that urbanization is generative of an emergent political order. It is one where the state recedes and urban collective life emerges as a significant political resource and location.

Building on this reformulation of politics in a context of urbanization, Chapter 3 details our understanding of democracy in relation to the city. We root our arguments in the radical democracy tradition, particularly the work of Sheldon Wolin, seeing democracy residing in practices and nurtured by shared political experiences. Following Wolin, democracy is understood as the process of building capacities of self-government in order to gain and maintain access to the urban common-wealth, and to share the social property of the city. The city is important for the project of urban democracy because, as a political idea, it can be used to situate democracy in concrete locations and to challenge the often alienated relations between people and places. We then engage with the democratic paradox of the state: that democracy can never be rooted in the state, but given the state's reach in contemporary societies it can never be avoided. To deal with this, we argue, following Simon Critchley, that democracy requires an interstitial distance to the state.

Chapters 4–6 consider different settings in order to delineate key aspects of an urban democracy in relation to the challenges it encounters. Chapter 4 takes the setting of the 'home', and housing struggles, to discuss the relations between urbanization and self-government, drawing contrasts between an urban and a state logic of democracy. We refer to a diversity of places (Barcelona, Berlin, Los Angeles, Zurich) and identify a range of locally specific political strategies for urban self-government. The key challenge we reflect on is that of making urban spaces amenable to self-government, pushing back against the state and market to enable a democratization of everyday life. This involves different means of knowledge production and political practice, from occupying empty buildings to developing capacity for the self-production of housing. Strategies of self-government vary according to context, but in all cases housing is an infrastructure and a means of appropriating and shaping urban transformations in their everyday guise.

Chapter 5 takes the wider setting of urban collective life to describe how political citizens emerge through urban publics. In the process it considers how the city can provide a way of locating collective organization and common cause in a fragmented world. We begin our discussion with Critical Mass to exemplify the conviction that there are urban publics already present and that they are difficult to grasp and comprehend through the dominant state-centred lens on politics. We then look at various examples of activism from around the globe, such as social centres and parallel institutions of urban food production and sanitation. We read such diverse practices as making matters of common concern public beyond the institutional gaze. We observe in these practices also a more confrontational politics, contesting exclusion and advancing forms of 'insurgent citizenship' based on belonging in the city.[66] Here urban collective life becomes an alternative horizon of democratic engagement, one of becoming an urban citizen by occupying and (re)making the spaces of the city. In this chapter, we detail how urbanites become subjects of urban transformations in mundane places and situations. They reshuffle socio-spatial relations without making claims for sovereignty. It is a specifically urban way of being/becoming political, where practices, objects, bodies and ideas are assembled in urban collective life and related to urbanization.

Chapter 6 explores the setting of the urban state to address the relation between an urban democracy reimagined and the institutions and practices of the state. As well as dealing with the problem of the state in relation to democracy, in this chapter we show that the state can be de-centred and turned into an enabler of urban self-government. The relations are always contingent and situated and so is the political strategy. To analyse these relations, we develop Critchley's idea that democratic projects must establish interstitial distances to the state. There is no clear-cut binary between state and society. Urban democracy is not confined to 'society' in opposition to the state. Rather, we articulate the state as a terrain of democratic struggle, with contingent and morphing reaches of power. We identify four interstitial distances to the state by looking critically at new municipalist projects in Europe (Barcelona, Naples, Preston) and the United States (Jackson, Mississippi). In these projects we detect practices of an activist yet non-sovereign state tackling the sources and outcomes of urbanization. These examples show that there is no one perfect way to deal with the state; instead they raise the vital question: to what purpose(s) can the state be put in democratic projects? Drawing on these examples, and with theories of radical democracy in mind, we conclude by arguing that an urban(ized) state would be adherent to the self-government of urban society, acknowledging its non-sovereignty and therefore seeking different modes of engagement with urbanites.

Chapter 7 concludes the book. We draw together our arguments and outline the project of an urban democracy reimagined, a resituating of the idea of what, where and how democracy can be. The democratic idea of the city is apparent in the examples in the book, we argue, as an idea defined by the urban as a contested terrain, the political situated in urban collective life, and democracy as a horizon of struggle for common cause and collective action. The state remains a key force in the politics of urbanization, but struggles for democratic urbanization transcend the political contestations and antagonisms articulated within institutions of governments at any scale. We end the book by emphasizing that urban democracy, from our perspective, becomes a project to rework and reshape socio-spatial practices and relations directly in urban collective life. The city as a shared idea of collective ownership and common practice is crucial for this project. It helps to forge alliances without falling into the local or communitarian trap. This is how the city can liberate democracy from the confines of the nation state and bring it back to the ordinary spaces where people live their lives.

2

Politics through an Urban Lens

In this book we ask how urbanization provides new political openings for a democracy in crisis. Our claim is a bold but well founded one. Urbanization changes the rules of the political game. This is not because cities as political jurisdictions become more important, nor is it because the planetary scope of urbanization turns all locations into urban settings. Rather, it is because urbanization contributes to a profound shift in the way politics is understood and practised. In order to really make sense of this transformation we have to broaden our scholarly perspectives on politics. Specifically, we must move away from the state as being the central actor in our account of how politics functions. Instead, by taking an *urban* view of politics we can discover the political possibilities urbanization can present. Of course, politics is conventionally understood as collating in national and international arenas, taking the form of the daily rigmarole of parliamentary debates and media appearances, punctuated by events like elections, performed through political parties competing for control of state institutions. But occasionally, if increasingly, this standard view is turned on its head by events. The outbreak of the Covid-19 pandemic in 2020 was one such occasion.

As health officials, scientists, governments and citizens grappled with the effects of the pandemic, the extent to which the urban shapes the world became very apparent to some. In the journal *Nature Sustainability*, an interdisciplinary team argued that in order to cope adequately with the crisis, it was necessary to see it 'through an urban lens'.[1] What did they mean by this? Political solutions needed to be thought of in terms of the places where most social production took place – within *urban collective life* situated in the urban everyday. This entailed thinking about global health governance through urban spaces and processes. Only by doing this was it possible to grasp the everyday rhythms, routines and encounters through which the world functions and which, as a result, make it possible for a pandemic to spread. Such insights were not possible through nation-state institutions, which are a mere part of the panoply of urban collective life but can never account for it. In other words, addressing the Covid-19 crisis through an urban lens meant de-centring the state and foregrounding the central role of citizens, neighbourhood organizations and other urban communities in terms of problem-solving initiatives as well as the articulation of the everyday problems confronting urban residents. It also implied a (re)situating of the 'national' (e.g. state institutions) and 'global' (e.g. economic processes), thinking of them in terms of their embeddedness in urban collective life. This shift in perspective was imperative for translating the complexity of the pandemic into matters of shared concern, which could then be dealt with politically. 'The urgency', the authors argued, 'to see like a city is clear'.

Despite such arguments, official responses to the pandemic remained largely stuck in the nation-state arena, comprehending the crisis through state-centric lenses and governmental machines. And with predictable outcomes. In their work on major cities in the global south, Gautam Bhan and colleagues showed that the nation state shaped responses that were of little benefit in mitigating the quotidian hardship caused by the pandemic.[2] They also foregrounded 'urban collective life' as the crucial entry point for responding to the pandemic, in order to understand the importance of urban everyday processes through which social life unfolds: 'Reading the pandemic through collective life means looking beyond formal actors and institutions, legible landscapes, neatly tabulated data, and linear economic rationalities. It is to acknowledge the reality and potential of the tacit ways in which people moved, acted and related with one another to produce urban outcomes.'[3]

Foregrounding urban collective life like this is a way of looking at politics through an urban lens. How do things change when we exchange the state lens for the urban lens? Well, for a start urban collective life looks quite different politically. Through an urban lens, neither planning nor policy is something disembodied from the individuals, communities and collectives affected. If the urban view is not about looking down, from the vantage point of the state, it is also not about looking up to the state, or elsewhere. It is about looking across and through social relations and material spaces to discern webs of politics and networks of power.[4] New registers and realms of politics come into view. Situated home-making practices and the life worlds of urbanites are no longer mere objects of policy-making or planning targeted by distant but powerful actors.[5] Instead, the urban provides the sources and places to build and to localize political capacity in the first place and to develop specific knowledges and practices to address shared place-based concerns. While such an urban lens should not obscure the power of the state, it brings the active role of citizens into view and the contingencies of urban spaces into relief. An urban understanding of the political does not rely on established and reified polities, but contributes to the emergence of a multiplicity of claims and publics.

This chapter considers the political potential of such an urban lens. Reflecting on key debates on urban politics, we argue that urbanization is generating a new political order where the urban everyday becomes a more crucial political locus. To begin, however, we briefly consider what we need to leave behind – the state lens on politics – and how we can do so.

Moving away from the state lens on politics

The state-centred view of politics has dominated the theory and practice of modern politics. The Oxford English Dictionary offers a definition of politics that most people probably intuitively share. The first entry reads: 'The activities associated with the governance of a country or area, especially the debate between parties having power.'[6] So, from this we can understand politics to be a specific constellation of collective organizations (i.e. parties) and how they rule a specified territory structured by traditional institutions of political systems. The subsections of this entry continue: 'The activities of governments concerning the political relations between states', and '[t]he academic study of government and the state'. For a term with ancient roots, this definition, focused on states and government, seems oddly ahistorical. Indeed, it is contingent on what scholars tell us we should think of as a historical formation, a politics particular to the conditions of a specific time and place.

A key assumption we make in this book is that politics, and democracy, are too often linked automatically and indelibly with what the political theorist Simon Tormey calls the period of 'high modernist' politics in the twentieth century.[7] This refers mainly to nations of the global north, representative democracies characterized by elections, the centrality of political parties and parliaments, all underpinned by massive state bureaucracies.[8] James C. Scott, who argued that this high modernist politics was not unique to liberal democracies in the global north, emphasized that it was a project of the nation, seen as the site of political governance designed to deal with conflicts and develop society. His famous 'Seeing Like a State' treatise asserted that state-centred modernist politics rests ultimately on a bird's-eye view of the world.[9] The logic of the state, in Scott's depiction, is a function of distancing political decision-making from specific places with distinct histories, traditions and perceptions. To see like a state is to order, administer, categorize and schematize territories, peoples, flows and goods, drawing on the seemingly self-evident advancement of science and technology. In the 'high-modernist ideology', as Scott calls it, the state's role was distinct from society, indeed the idea was to act upon societies, from a vantage point, in an expansive and encompassing way.

Viewed through a state lens on politics, urban collective life appears as something apart, an object to be perceived and grasped through policy and planning, something to which power should be applied. Of course, there are variations between countries and systems. Yet, the modern understanding of the state is associated with the concentration of knowledge and rules in state administrations, the consolidation of sources of domination and violence in police and military organizations, as well as the struggle for power through periodic elections. The statist way of thinking about how societies organize themselves to address matters of public concern has become dominant even though, as David Graeber and David Wengrow have argued, it is ultimately a system of hierarchies and institutions, which more often reinforces inequalities instead of making alternatives possible.[10]

This state-centred framework is only one version of what politics and democracy are and can be. It is one way of looking at the world. But it remains a potent one, reinforced in academic and political debates.[11] Alternative visions of politics that are not centred on the state and its institutions, but look for politics in other locations, are often dismissed or denigrated as 'anti-political', when often they might simply be 'anti' a particular way of doing politics, rather than seeking to deny politics per se.[12] Warren Magnusson, whose work has achieved so much in wresting politics away from the state lens, put it well when he stated that much of what seemed like the main show of politics in nineteenth-century Europe – the so-called high politics of statecraft and diplomacy – now seems fairly irrelevant in relation to what happened on the streets and in the backrooms where diverse democratic ideas and movements emerged.[13] Hence, the lesson to be learnt was not to follow the usual paths which lead to great institutions and figures. 'If we keep looking for politics in the places where it used to be, we may soon discover that the world has passed us by.'[14] The implication is clear: in an urbanizing world, we need to shrug off the state lens on politics.

A first step in doing this is to think of politics as a form of societal action, no doubt encompassing but always exceeding the state. Looking across diverse writings on politics, such a definition might begin with the characteristics of possibility and struggles over collective futures. Colin Hay states that politics is 'the capacity for agency and deliberation in situations of genuine collective or social choice'.[15] Magnusson asserts that '[t]o speak of politics is to invoke the domain of human possibility: a world of judgement, choice, and action'.[16] Inevitably, then, politics pertains to power, to who wins and loses,[17] and political power can be generated (through mobilization) as well as unleashed (from institutional resources); it is not merely about decision-making power, but about shaping contexts and patterns of thought and action.[18] Elmer Schattschneider thought of politics in terms of 'the conflict of conflicts' – the broader, foundational contest by which more particular contests appear – and the capacities of political agents to engage in this conflict.[19] In classical political thought, politics is about developing collective ways of ruling and governing, as in Aristotle's *Politics*.[20] But there can be no satisfactory definition which avoids differences and contests. Indeed, contests are productive of politics, moving the very ground upon which it stands, and they have formed the theoretical core of post-foundational political philosophy.[21] Yet, if we think of it in terms of agency and contingency, shaping the worlds we inhabit, politics does not boil down to conflict alone. Politics can unfold in a variety of forms, take shape in diverse strategies and practices, and it can be just as much about solidarities as conflict, as much about friendship as hostility.[22]

In an age increasingly shaped by urbanization rather than the nation state, we should, then, seek out the key political struggles to shape the urban. Yet, the theoretical roots of much thinking on urban politics (as well as democracy) are also burdened by the state and its relation to the 'city'. Usually, the political character of the city is seen as an effect of statehood established within the boundaries of a clearly defined political entity. The city is seen as an embryo-like nation state. The Greek polis is of course the best-known case, but the European mediaeval city-states (like Florence and Venice) provide further examples. In this view, the polis is political because it is administered by (para-)state bodies. But what if the political character of the city is an effect of its urban condition and not of its state structures? Following Magnusson, this is to see politics not in a realm formally separate from society (i.e. the state), but rather embedded in the social-material world around us, in the everyday things we do.[23]

Magnusson has called this 'Seeing Like a City', drawing a contrast with Scott's 'Seeing Like a State'.[24] This shift from a state-centric view to an urban lens is at first glance one of concepts and language. Yet it has empirical and normative consequences. Looking through an urban lens, new empirical phenomena come to the fore, while others recede. What is more, how we as observers and scholars tell the story of how urbanites respond to spatial and social transformation differs depending on the lenses we use. In normative terms, we can shed light on and validate a politics often overlooked in public debates. This politics is not simply about city elites, business owners, elected officials and civil servants, and how they build coalitions to achieve urban development and order. Instead, what emerges is the crucial role of localized action by urbanites and how they mobilize around day-to-day issues. The urban view is one from within the thick of things, crowded by life rather than apart from it. 'To see the political through the city is to notice how proximate diversity stimulates self-organization and self-government, generates politics in and between authorities in different registers, and defers the sovereignty claims it produces', as Magnusson puts it.[25] Hence, the urban should not be understood in terms of more or less distinct topographical locations that one can situate on a map. Rather, the urban – and, as we will go on to argue, the city – is a way of looking at and acting upon the world in which one is located.

We find traces and seeds of these ideas in many debates on urban politics in the past and the present. On a most basic level, scholars agree that there is something specific about politics when it 'happens' in the city or in an urban context. For some it is the constraints that the city and political actors are faced with. Alternatively, as Allan Cochrane has convincingly argued, the urban can be seen as a series of particular settings – social, economic, racial, material and so on – which are politically generative. In this view, the *urban* in urban politics stands for distinct problems that occur, the distinct actors that might organize around these problems, and the distinct conflicts that may unfold.[26] Taking this perspective, the urban can be 'unbound', seen as a socio-material, multidimensional process, or moments therein, which not only produce specific demands and a politics around these demands, but also a different logic and plane of political action.[27] This politics of the urban does not override other perspectives on urban politics but emphasizes urban collective life as a political space outside the confines of formal state-centric politics. To get to this point, however, it is instructive to consider how urban politics has been debated, in order to emphasize both the steps needed to see politics through an urban lens and to consider the range of consequences thereof.[28]

The politics of the urban

Urban politics, conventionally understood, is in the first instance synonymous with city or town hall politics, focused on the main state institutions designed to rule with legal jurisdiction at the local or city scale. This politics may not be just about local issues, especially as globalization advances, nor only about the workings of the local state, as 'multi-level' interaction has always been apparent in towns and cities, given their importance to social and economic life. Still, this is 'subnational' politics, as the discipline of political science tells us, with the clear implication that politics becomes more contentious and important – more *political* as it were – when it reaches the national level. Peter John encapsulates this view: 'urban politics is about authoritative decision-making at a smaller scale than national units ... The urban is politics in miniature and this creates a particular kind of political system rather than a mirror image of other levels, largely to do with smaller numbers of the elite and the ease at which its members can interact.'[29] In this view, the form politics takes in the urban is similar to those at other scales. It is about articulating political demands through electoral venues, shaped by actors seeking to influence political decision-making in state institutions. Of course, these interests are not equal, and accounts of urban politics often seem more vividly to capture the fragility of state institutions in the face of economic might.

In the canonical political science accounts of city politics, the focus is on a politics of representation, the interests, resources and influence (or not) of local elites, and the means by which political leaders forge coalitions around urban policy agendas. Depending on the empirical focus and research interest, either the power distribution or the workings of the inner circle of the political elite come into view. In Robert Dahl's well-known 1961 text, *Who Governs? Democracy and Power in an American City*, the pluralist contest over votes and organizational support is foregrounded.[30] In the case of Dahl's book, but also other classical texts, such as Floyd Hunter's *Community Power Structure: A Study of Decision Makers* (1953), the fulcrum of urban politics is the institutional arena of the (local) state and the actors who have access to this arena. In the political science tradition of urban politics there is often a particular focus on personalities and political office, to the extent that they are relevant to questions of governance.[31]

A focus on elected officials, economic elites and bureaucrats has its merits. Without doubt, these are the actors who usually dispose of the means necessary to develop and enact policy agendas. They have the institutional power to build support. They also have the political legitimacy and financial resources to implement urban development projects at a large scale. What is more, the state – be it local, regional or national – often has the means and power to hold back those forces that seek to challenge and transform urban politics as usual. However, this perspective on politics has been challenged in at least two key ways. First, what seems particular about the urban setting is that electoral politics is conditioned by external and internal limits. Urban elites operate in constrained and changing environments where they need to seek support and resources outside the electoral institutions of the city. Second, this perspective overlooks the complexity of urban life and how it is generative of politics in terms of demands but also in terms of distinct actors and coalitions. So, one might wonder what is being overlooked when the lens remains trained on elections, businesses and elites alone: what politics do we fail to see?[32]

The external constraints on city hall politics are manifest. In his influential 1981 book, *City Limits*, Paul Peterson argued that, due to mobile capital, cities have a 'unitary interest' in developmental policies.[33] Economic competition between cities constrains the policy options at hand, and this shapes politics in the sense that some demands are simply excluded because of their (assumed) detrimental economic effects. This is, of course, a rather deterministic view of urban politics. However, it captures an idea that is still widespread in urban debates, namely that cities are faced with particular socio-material conditions or forces, now mainly concentrated in the global economy, that may vary between cities but ultimately impose a 'politics of inevitability' on city hall and electoral politics.[34] This politics takes the form of urban governance where *entrepreneurialism* is the dominant logic: that to survive in a competitive economic environment city governments have to actively animate development and growth in the private sector. As a result, city governments are ever more embedded in a 'web of institutional, economic, and political constraints which create a set of contingencies in the process of governing', meaning they need to forge coalitions with societal actors to address problems, dealing strategically with the limits of their authority.[35]

If Dahl's purpose was to find out who governs cities and to what ends, academics since have increasingly painted a picture of urban politics in which the power of the state to govern is more contingent upon a range of actors beyond formal institutions and arenas and also more subservient to the global economy. The impact of external constraints – or the construction of such constraints in the first place – on urban politics and how scholars think about it has been ever more pronounced with the acceleration of global urbanization. Concepts such as Urban Regimes, Growth Machines or Urban Governance emphasize the necessity, in the absence of a truly sovereign (local) state, of building broad governing coalitions around policy agendas.[36]

Research on Urban Regimes has shown that governing the urban is dependent on a range of different actors and resources coming together in tight alliances. The socially productive side of power is often but not always much more important than the sovereign force or the power over others. Hence, in this literature, governmental or state actors are conceived differently on the urban level to their counterparts on the national level. While at least in ideal-typical terms the state on the national level is conceived as sovereign and less dependent on non-governmental actors, the state on the urban or local level can hardly claim sovereignty as it is always already enmeshed with the non-governmental sphere. However, this does not imply that the urban state is equally open to different organizations and collaborations. Urban governments react to selective incentives that often reproduce the existing inequalities and power relations embedded in economic and social life. The porosity of the urban or local state does not result per se in more progressive or emancipatory governing arrangements. And building capacity to act is not conditioned by electoral gains. These analyses point to the intricate transnational webs of political governance in which states now operate, and to the fragmentation and informalization of political authority across transnational spaces.[37]

Such academic debate suggests that what makes the urban a specific political system is that it cannot be reduced to formal politics because electoral arenas and elected officials are constrained in various ways in what they can do. However, the understanding of urban politics is still essentially defined by governmental actions and their institutional reach. These approaches differ in their accounts of where and how governments should be organized and where and how they should build coalitions or regimes. But what they share is a rather limited view of the urban as a source of political potential. This is because the state view of urban politics leads to a primary understanding of the urban as a category of governmental action and policy intervention.

There is, however, another stream of foundational debates on urban politics which claims that the urban as socio-material space is also productive and generative of politics. Here the urban is not merely the socio-material density, proximity and heterogeneity seen as characteristic of cities. Instead, urbanization as a process and the urban as a specific condition generate economic and social relations and problems of public concern, but also different *urban* resources and forms of organizations to address them. The urban and urbanization move from the neutral background of politics to centre stage as shapers of interests, opportunities and demands.

Manuel Castells' work is instructive in this regard.[38] Underlying the urban question he posed in the 1970s was the assumption that the urban provides significant and specific conditions of being political because it is where the problematic of collective consumption crystallizes. In the 1980s, Castells outlined a terrain of politics in which a new political subject – urban social movements – entered the scene, for which the urban with its different sources, realities and infrastructures (and not, say, class, gender or race) was foundational.[39] Urban social movements have been confrontational to governments but they have also maintained various relations to local electoral politics. At the same time they can be seen as operating increasingly in lived spaces of the urban. Their activities have been concerned with addressing encompassing societal problems, but they have pursued multiple strategies in diverse urban spaces. This is a politics far from the chambers of city hall (even if the latter remains a central preoccupation): a politics of protest, of people in numbers occupying symbolic places in the city, such as the main squares and streets, organizing on the ground.

What Castells and others grasped was the significance of spaces of politics and the material conditions of struggles.[40] This perspective delivers a theory of social change and politics in which the urban is not just a neutral institutional frame but a political source and stake, to be considered akin to class, race or gender. Understood in this sense, urbanization and the urban are productive forces shaping not only the built environment but also economic interests, opportunities and threats, a sense of belonging and identity, and (re)sources of political mobilization and subjectivation.[41] This also implies that all actors, forces and organizations who shape or are being shaped by urbanization can become important politically. In this view, urban politics is not restricted to city hall, nor to class interests and the factory floor. The key contribution made by Castells, drawing on Henri Lefebvre, was to shift political action into the realm of urban collective life. However, he rendered the urban 'passive', to use Andy Merrifield's description, just as it was about to become the very stake of capitalist production as globalization advanced in the 1980s and 1990s and the state, in general terms, became more aligned with capital interests.[42] Urban politics remained in the state frame, with the state as the dominant organizational principle and set of institutional actors – at different levels – still key as a stage and horizon of political struggles. Hence, while the issues may have been distinctly urban, they were treated in the fashion of the state. The state was not just an organizational principle setting the scene, allocating roles and defining the rules of the game; it was also a temporal and spatial order of the political.

What we propose in the next section is that the distinctly *urban* character of urban politics deviates from the organizational principle of the state, since it foregrounds different spaces and agencies of the political embedded in the urban everyday and recognizable as urban collective life. The urban everyday, we claim, is not just a phenomenological entry point for capturing urban life; it is also a way of looking at how urbanites resonate in political ways with their environment and its transformation. The urban everyday is not passive, the outcome of other processes (of capital, or state intervention), but is rather the realm in which urbanization can become politically productive (or not): it is a site, source and stake in politics. When we take the urban everyday as the plane of a different, distinctly urban politics, other arenas and players come into focus which also have the ability to mobilize resources and effect change. Their resources, however, may differ from a state-centric view, and the agendas around which they mobilize are entwined with their day-to-day lives.

The urbanization of politics

Global urbanization is a political game-changer. Numerous scholars tell us that the 'urban' is not only increasingly potent, but also amorphous, disrupting accepted categories and generating new social meaning. The old rules are still in play, but they are pencilled rather than inked in, not always corresponding to politics in diverse urban contexts. In the following, we will argue that planetary urbanization undermines not only well-established spatial categories but also the centrality of the political authority of the state. To be clear, we are not claiming that the state is no longer important as a political, social and economic engine. The state is still a key player, able to collect and distribute large amounts of resources, be they financial, natural, human or intellectual. But the state has also undergone a process of informalization. In the process, the urban everyday and urban collective life emerge as a plane and organizational principle of politics with different potentialities.

Intensified urbanization blurs the concepts and terms of ordinary language: what is urban or rural, global or local, is no longer clear. This is the claim made in the book *New Urban Worlds* by Simone and Pieterse, one of the most striking recent interventions in urban studies.[43] The urban, as they vividly describe, is productive – it is an animating force. The socio-materiality of the urban, while subject to and often becalmed by the forces of the state and market, nevertheless has a proclivity to unruliness. The urban is always a meeting and mix of human agency, material forms (like utility infrastructure, built form), physical landscape and climatic conditions. In a similar vein, Ash Amin and Nigel Thrift argue that a collective performance of sorts takes place between these various elements to generate and stabilize (or not) urban spaces of diverse densities, velocities, meanings and activities.[44] While these elements can be and often are assembled in an effort to ensure security and predictability, the fact that the urban is dependent on lots of bits and pieces aligning makes it very contingent. Small acts (or withdrawals) can have major repercussions. Aligning political forces have many routes available to them, which encompass the diversity of material urban worlds rather than focusing on formal institutions of state and market as realms apart from them.

From Simone's and Pieterse's perspective the differences between local and global, public and private, exterior and interior, intensive and extensive blur, but often in concussive ways that generate tensions. It is through these tensions, fissures and notches that new objects and subjects emerge loaded with political meaning. What Simone and Pieterse observe is that while the traditional rules of politics are still in view, in terms of policy and political action, their power to shape and resonate with urban collective life is diminished. When we look for a different politics in which the urban is 'the condition of possibility for the political',[45] we will find fragmented power and the political rationale of self-government – not as a humanistic utopia but rather as a pragmatic and liberating practice. In a similar vein, Brenner and Schmid state that the 'urban' should be understood as 'a collective project', generated through struggle, experimentation and negotiation within the context of global or planetary urbanization. Crucial to its possibility, the urban offers 'an open horizon in relation to which concrete struggles over the urban are waged'.[46]

In another key recent intervention, Julie-Anne Boudreau asserts that because of planetary urbanization, our experience, affects and logics of action are increasingly shaped and conditioned by the urban situations we find ourselves in.[47] 'Living in an urban world', she writes, 'affects how we act politically because the spaces, temporalities and rationalities of action differ from what dominated a world of nation states'.[48] A driving force behind this move to 'a specifically urban way of acting politically'[49] is the informalization of the state. The nation state and sovereignty do not lie at the core of *global urban politics*. However, the state is not gone altogether and the focus of politics should not just be the 'outside' of formal state institutions. Rather, the informalization induced by urbanization might also transform the very idea and practice of the state in an emergent political order. Boudreau's conception of an urban logic of political action foregrounds urbanity, the 'here and now', as it occurs in 'networked, fluid and mobile spaces' and 'escapes the reach of, and is not directed towards, the geographically bounded state'.[50]

Boudreau's work forces us to be mindful of the multifaceted nature of, and the temporal and spatial conjunctures between, the urban and political. Lefebvre's foregrounding of *everyday life* as the terrain of political contestation is helpful here. For Lefebvre the everyday is not just mundane, daily life. Rather, he understands the everyday as a distinct space structured by routines apart from specialized activities (i.e. work, politics, etc.) governed by urbanization.[51] Everyday life is indeed key for the reproduction of the economy and society more generally because it is in the sphere of the everyday that desires are formed and articulated and contradictions felt and normalized. From this perspective, 'the everyday is the very soil on which the great architecture of politics and society rise up'.[52] At the same time, the plane of the everyday provides political opportunities to break with the everydayness of life and to relate to transformative political and economic projects.[53]

The importance of the urban everyday as a phenomenological object and as a way to grasp and understand contemporary urban life has also been revealed from other standpoints in urban scholarship. Most notably, the postcolonial literature has been particularly crucial in providing a sense of the political import of urban everyday situations and the everyday practices employed to improvise, make ends meet and make life viable.[54] Here the urban exists in the often unseen or overlooked practices of the everyday, and politics lies in the potential to re-imagine and re-work it. A key argument has centred on 'the undecidability of the urban',[55] and the extent to which it is realized, contested and negotiated in the plane of the everyday.

Postcolonial writers have developed new concepts of political action, removed from direct confrontation or domination, and fundamentally located in the everyday. Of particular note is Bayat's concept of the non-mobilization and non-organization of collective politics in 'nonmovements'.[56] He shows that urban daily life in the Middle East often generates the possibility of political mobilizations that defer sovereignty claims and challenge the natural order of the city. Scholars focused on the global north have also taken inspiration from the postcolonial turn to re-ground urban politics in the everyday, exposing informality and foregrounding everyday practices.[57] Alexander Vasudevan has conceived the political possibilities of the urban in terms of the 'makeshift city', in which the informal, precarious practices of squatting might act as a 'touchstone for other alternative imaginings of cityness'.[58]

The urban, then, has a political potential that is not only apart from the state, but is sometimes unfindable and unreadable by state institutions. Bodies, ideas and collectives are assembled and related to the urban and urbanization in the everyday. But what of the state and market? The everyday and the regulatory authority of the capitalist and state organization of space are not separate registers. Rather, they are interdependent because top-down spatial organization always relies on the everyday practices sustaining it.[59] Hence, the urban everyday contains a latent political power and possibility. In the everyday, ways of thinking and doing things can be addressed and ultimately challenged by counter-claims.[60]

This shift to the everyday has implications for our understanding of urban politics. Urban politics no longer belongs in a box (mark as applicable): scale, space, jurisdictional remit.[61] Instead, power is assembled and requires place-based articulations; however, because power is displaced across these networks it has a vulnerability, which creates opportunities for contestation. Furthermore, because the urban can shift, with the potential for new connections to emerge quickly and across disparate urban spaces, it also has a kinetic power, which is crucial to its political potential.[62] We have seen this latter quality – and its limits – in urban uprisings like those in Egypt during the Arab Spring, where the urban ignites, takes on an energy, which can challenge embedded forms of power. Hence, the urban can be seen as a multitude of performances and outcomes, which can generate huge power when they align, but which remain inherently contingent and subject to change. This means that politics runs through the urban, even if the urban is not, in every space, place or experience, political.

The city in urban politics

If the urban is contested, generated through collective everyday practices, and a process rather than a fixed form, where does this leave one of the most historically significant spatial understandings of politics – the 'city'? Ever since Plato outlined the ideal polis, or city-state, in *The Republic*, political theory has tended to assume a mutual condition of possibility between the 'urban' and 'politics'. In practice, particularly since the industrialization and urbanization of the nineteenth century, the city and its streets (e.g. Paris, 1871) and squares (e.g. Tahir Square, 2011) have been pivotal to the course of world (not just 'urban') politics. But in a context of global urbanization does the 'city' still mean something politically?[63]

Scholars have shown that the dominance of global corporations in relation to political decision-making has advanced politics as a function of management (of social and individual demands), rather than as a stage for contests about future worlds.[64] These concerns were translated into the field of urban studies.[65] Drawing on diverse writers in the field of post-foundational political thought, Erik Swyngedouw observed an urban politics exhumed of the truly political, constructed through empty signifiers like the 'global city' or the 'creative city'. His 'post-political city' is one in which the historical link between the city and politics is hanging by a thread.[66] Hence, the urban becomes depoliticized as a result of broader political change, the effects of a post-political order. This perspective transformed the debate on urban politics, bringing renewed urgency to questions of democratic possibility; at the same time, however, the 'post-political city' thesis took a narrow view of urban politics, abstaining from a theoretical engagement with urbanization as a politically productive process.[67] This contrasts with many other strands in the recent literature, where scholars ask where urban politics is to be found, what forms of politics might emerge in urban settings, and how, ultimately, the particularities of the city can still be crucial in shaping political visions and practices in a context of global urbanization.[68]

'The city' as well as 'the urban' are heavily contested as viable analytical categories to capture these uneven and heterogeneous processes of urbanization, and there is disagreement as to how researchers should cope with these terms 'after the age of the city'.[69] Some argue that we should dismiss the urban and the city as categories altogether, or, at least, plead for a fundamental reframing.[70] Others, however, claim the still universal significance of the city and reassert that it is not only feasible but also necessary to develop a general theory of the nature of cities as a 'distinctive, concrete social phenomenon'.[71] Against this background, we insist that the concept of the 'city' is still politically productive – not as a singular spatial form, or a set of spatial markers of political productivity, but as a foundation for political imagination and action.[72]

Later chapters in the book shed light on the political productivity of the 'city'. What is important to say here is that the idea and practice of the city provide a means to grasp urbanization as it is articulated by citizens themselves. This implies thinking of the city in terms of how residents, commuters, administrators, businessmen and activists make sense of urbanization processes, how they represent and situate them in political terms. As Azam Khatam and Oded Haas have argued, the city as a 'political construct, is crucial for understanding how the "urban" is produced, challenged and reclaimed by everyday life'.[73] The city is a political horizon, a site where struggles are situated and brought into relation with other struggles. What is more, and as we will address in the next chapter, the city can also be conceived as the very stake of democratic politics. As Roger Keil argues persuasively, in an urbanized world, urbanites are increasingly making claims to their part of the urban world: their right to access, enjoy and profit from the resources and values of urbanity they co-produce through their labour, their engagement in everyday life and their contribution to urban spaces.[74]

Political openings

To sum up our key arguments in this chapter: urbanization is generative of an emergent political order, where the city as a category of practice remains key to politicizing urbanization. To grasp the political openings of urbanization we need to shift our view away from the state towards the urban as an alternative terrain of politics shaping the local knowledges, practices and ambitions of urbanites across the globe. Although the form, extent and impact of urban political practices varies across contexts, we can think of politics in terms of a general move away from institutions of the state (as friend or enemy) into multiple urban locations. This marks a descent from the perch of modernist politics and a confrontation with diverse urban political practices at eye level. Politics viewed through an urban lens is less shaped by the procedures of state bureaucracy and political decision-making and more entwined with the practices of everyday life, the creation of new spaces of action, and processes of individual and collective reproduction.[75] Only through such a shift might we discover an emergent political order in the urban, one encompassing multiple spatialities of claims to self-government coming from the home, from the streets, from services and even, but not exclusively, from city hall. New political actors enter the scene, capable of mobilizing distinct urban resources and assembling the collectives necessary not only to keep the city running but also to build and realize alternative political agendas.[76]

The urban view of politics expands the conception of the political, spatially and temporally, as well as in terms of practices and aims beyond winning or protesting state power.[77] This means taking the conditions of urban collective life seriously and allowing for a broader spectrum of political activity. Furthermore, if the urban and the city become a stake, site and source of politics, then this, in turn, suggests a range of political strategies:

- Adopting neither a micro nor a grand politics, but focusing on urban collective life, urbanites might establish forms of local self-government and political authority at one remove, entirely disconnected from, or even toe-to-toe with, the formal institutions of urban governance. In other words, this type of political action goes beyond a binary understanding of the state-society relation. Rather, it attempts to pluralize political authority in cities.

- Hence, an *urban* politics explores the potential for political and economic self-governance, not sovereignty. It is not primarily related to binding collective decision-making formalized in laws and regulation. Instead, it is much more concerned with situating struggles in actual urban spaces, where inequalities and grievances emerge and where people come together based on matters of shared concern. Situated urban struggles rest upon local knowledges and relations, and have the potential to remain accessible to groups that are often politically excluded within urban society.
- Taking the city as a category of political practice, and urban collective life as a political locus, foregrounds the particular political strategy of eroding, rather than escaping, taming or smashing, capitalism as it intrudes on current forms of urbanism.[78] The means of erosion are the politicization and transformation of urban spaces, and intervention in the practices of urban collective life.

In sum, this emergent political order of the urban must call into question long-held conventions about democracy, and force us to look at democracy through an urban lens. We cannot expect an urban democracy to be confined to well-known spaces such as parliaments and squares; indeed, we will need to think how it is extended through urban space. If elections and policy-making will not stand centre stage in an urban democracy, what will take their place? How will we identify urban forms of democracy? We turn to these questions in the next chapter.

3

Democracy and the City Reimagined

In this chapter we describe what we mean by democracy and why we think the city is important in current struggles for democracy. An epistemological theme running through this book is the back and forth between the practices and projects we observe in urbanized spaces across the globe, and the terms and concepts we use to describe them and make sense of how they might shape a more democratic future. The urban democracy we call for here is already apparent in many urban areas, if only in fragments. Urban citizens around the globe practise collective self-government of urban spaces or are fighting for it. The practices of self-government we see and describe in the coming chapters are often situated at a certain distance to more institutionalized arenas of collective decision-making. Because of that they can fall outside of what is usually conceived of as democratic politics. However, they articulate a distinct democratic vision based on the ideas of urban space as a common-wealth, and of urban collective life as politically resourceful. These citizens and collectives contest their exclusion or expulsion from the governance of the places where they live. They demand to be included in the urban common-wealth to which they contribute. In these practices we see a new democracy project, one that stands in tension with dominant understandings of democracy because it values doing (practices) over deferring (institutions) and morphing political collectives (urban demos) over pre-given communities (nation, ethnicity, etc.).[1] The city provides the actual and virtual space to situate and practise this project of democracy in contrast to the nation and in relation to global urbanization.

To be clear, the aim here is not to discover a new definition of democracy, nor is it to develop a model of democracy. Rather, we want to make sense of a variety of practices, collectives and ambitions that have emerged in different urban places over recent years. To comprehend what is happening on the ground, so to speak, we take our cue from the theoretical tradition of radical democracy. In this strand of thought, democracy is understood as a sphere of tensions, in which democracy itself can never be settled but is an ongoing project of finding common cause and organizing collective life worlds. Democracy in this perspective is an ongoing political struggle rather than an institutional framework. From this radical perspective, arrangements of collective self-organization are democratic to the extent that they embody a democratic ethos which regards the contingency and openness of politics as unavoidable and affirmatively necessary.[2] Further, the democratic ethos which guides this book strives for equality through the articulation of and actions towards common concerns and demands.[3] Democratic life based on this ethos encourages people to formulate their own and their shared troubles, and to establish spaces to debate their demands with other people in public. This is a politics doubtful of authorities, opposed to relations of domination, and prepared to challenge naturalized rules and norms in society. The democratic ethos which we profess is nurtured by situated practices and experiments that build common political experiences and democratic knowledge. Knowledge about democracy, and the multiple ways of practising democracy, is established in specific places and built from the ground up, discursively rather than top down. Ultimately, this democratic ethos is grounded on an openness, an understanding that 'ordinary individuals are capable of creating new cultural patterns of commonality at any moment'.[4] When these democratic moments occur, individuals are acting in concert with others and 'contributing to the discovery, care, and tending of a commonality of shared concerns'.[5]

Devising an urban model of democracy would contradict this ethos, denying the contingent openness at its core. Instead, our objective is to reflect on how a variety of struggles and practices in and against global urbanization can assume democratic meaning, despite being, or precisely because they are, beyond institutionalized forms. A model is not apparent, but a distinctly urban logic of democracy is: a process of advancing self-government through and for urban collectives claiming their right to the city, i.e. to access, enjoy, co-produce and benefit from urban space and urban life. As understood here, urban democracy is about the recurrent struggle to democratize urbanization. As will be shown, this still entails engaging with the state; but more importantly, it requires developing democracy at interstitial distances to the state.

Radical democracy

What do we mean when we talk about democracy? What are we striving for with our demands for more democracy? There is no single categorical answer to these questions. On the one hand, everybody seems to be in favour of democracy; or, at least, few disparage it in public. In this sense, core elements of democracy, such as collective self-government, equality and liberty, are taken-for-granted values necessary for a political system to be legitimate.[6] On the other hand, it seems very difficult to get to a shared understanding of what form of politics is favourable to advance these values or the democratic ethos we referred to above.

We have grown accustomed to discussing democracy in relation to the nation state. National elections have become the linchpin of contemporary democracy, the barometer by which to gauge its presence and monitor its health. The decline of local and regional party organizations and media outlets in many places has contributed to an intensification of political activity at the national level. Indeed, political commentators and most political scientists would want us to believe that the public sphere, if it exists, is scaled nationally, tightly knit to state and governmental actors as well as media platforms, and temporally structured by the electoral cycle. National democracies are based on liberal and constitutional ideas of democracy. In this view, the country (geography), the people (society) and the nation state (politics) provide the building blocks for a rather limited narrative about democracy. Key to this narrative is the claim that the state defined by institutions and grounded in constitutions is the proper and privileged political space for democratic engagement. Further, through the principle of representation on the input side, and administrative procedures on the output side, the nation and the demos are related to the institutional order of the state.

The tradition of radical democracy theory offers a very different perspective. Here, the idea that democracy can be defined through a distinct institutional form is a non-starter. There are of course different strands and emphases in radical democracy theory, but what they share is the conviction that confining democracy to certain institutional forms does not do justice to the meanings and possibilities of democracy.[7] From a radical democratic position, democracy is not (only) about institutionalizing equality and freedom. Rather, democratic engagement should articulate these strong normative ideas in a permanent struggle to democratize democracy.[8] As such, democracy has to be constantly interrogated as to what extent it allows these ideas to be realized. Despite the differences within the tradition, a radical vision of democracy strives for intense and permeating practices of self-government which should not and cannot be limited to certain domains, scales or areas of public life.[9] Hence, political institutions are always understood as means for, even moments within, the ongoing process of democratization, and not as its goal or limit. This implies that all political institutions, norms and values are open to scrutiny. This is the post-foundationalist backbone of radical democratic theory, the sense that there can be no closure or completion in society.[10]

One consequence of this standpoint is that the relation between the demos, the people striving for democracy, and the institutions that ultimately give democracy a certain form, stand in permanent and unresolvable tension. So there is a paradox inherent to democracy: the impossibility of it taking on a specific socio-political form, while being still dependent on some socio-political form in order to come into being. In other words, the rule of the people, collective self-government, cannot be prescribed:

> In some sense ... the 'people' are always undecidedly present and absent from the scenes of democracy. That is why it is always part of the point of democratic political practice to call them into being, rhetorically and materially, while acknowledging that such calls never fully succeed and invariably also produce remnants.[11]

The principle of democracy – in contrast to other forms of rule and authority – is that it accepts the ethos that there is no definite social foundation or hierarchy to rely upon. Democracy is contingent and open because no single agency nor any single group can claim divine or natural authority. This is the emancipatory potential of democracy. There is always the possibility of mobilizing different versions and ideas of the demos against those who claim to represent the demos. Hence, the tension between democratic politics as it is – realized through sovereign states and representative governments – and the democratic promise – realized through the demos – is unresolvable.

In theories of radical democracy there is some disagreement as to how this tension can be articulated in real world politics. The debate about the post-political city (as mentioned in Chapter 2) has been revealing in this regard.[12] The starting point of the debate was, and still is, that, over the last two decades or so, the democratic tension between reality and promise has been obscured by governments locked into a post-political consensus backed by political, economic and civic elites. As a result, democracy in a fundamental sense has been hollowed out and replaced by the depoliticized decision-making of bureaucratic bodies, interrupted by ceremonial events, like elections, and populist moments, which provide the appearance of political contest and democracy, but ultimately offer little choice or prospect of change. There is more or less agreement on this state of affairs amongst writers in the radical democracy tradition. Differences emerge with regard to the political strategy that might be fruitful to overcome the post-political condition and city. A 'dissociative' strand of the radical democracy tradition sees agonistic (or even antagonistic) confrontations as the only way to disrupt the existing political order and revive democracy. By contrast, the 'associative' strand claims that there is (still) the possibility of coming together in the public realm to form a political collective around shared concerns, which, through recurrent practices, can then revive democracy and political life.[13] While the dissociative strand thinks that democracy can only be realized and rescued through acts confronting the dominant political order institutionalized in states and government, the associative thinkers argue that democracy can come to fruition and eventually alter the political order through shared practices and experiences.

Sheldon Wolin's work can be positioned in the associative strand; it provides, for us, a very inspiring attempt to hold in suspension the lack of a democratic reality and the hope of the democratic promise. Democracy as the practice of acting together for the common good generates the political experiences necessary for standing against anti-democratic tendencies. These practices and experiences can be short-lived, even momentary, but for Wolin they strive for a lasting transformation of the political order. In his critical reflection on the work of the liberal theorist John Rawls, Wolin presents a general idea of how he understands democracy:

> Democracy should not depend on elites making a onetime gift to the demos of a predesigned framework of equal rights. This does not mean that rights do not matter a great deal, but rights in a democracy depend on the demos winning them, extending them substantively, and, in the process, acquiring experience of the political, that is, of participating in power, reflecting on the consequences of its exercise, and struggling to sort out the common wellbeing amid cultural differences and socioeconomic disparities. The presence of democracy is not signified by paying deference to a formal principle of popular sovereignty but by ensuring continuing political education, nor is democracy nurtured by stipulating that reasonable principles of justice be in place from the beginning. Democracy requires that the experiences of justice and injustice serve as moments for the demos to think, to reflect, perchance to construct themselves as actors. Democracy is about the continuing self-fashioning of the demos.[14]

What is appealing in this quotation, and throughout Wolin's work, is his emphasis on democracy as a meaningful and shared practice and experience. Wolin is perhaps best known for his concept of a 'fugitive democracy', the idea that democracy can only be experienced temporarily or momentarily and needs to be actualized time and again.[15] Through this lens, the search for a definitive form for democracy contradicts the very substance of democracy conceived in terms of open-ended and vital practices. For Wolin, democracy is something other than a form of government. It is a 'mode of being', a way to experience and shape the common world.[16] The issue with democracy is that this mode of existence is fugitive and temporarily lost. Democracy as practice, then, always involves a mobilization and struggle to reinvent and re-establish it against counter and containing forces.

Given this line of reasoning, it comes as no surprise that Wolin has often been (mis)read as an American Jacques Rancière, who also emphasizes the emergent and ephemeral character of the political and democracy. But in contrast to Rancière, Wolin argues that 'democracy's fugitive or episodic tendencies are the great problem or "trouble" with democracy – not its great advantage, nor the source of purity or authenticity'.[17] Wolin's interests lay in the cultivation of a democratic consciousness, in how citizens might establish new cultural and political patterns supportive of democracy. He wrote about the United States, but his arguments resonate more widely with other nation-state forms of democracy – what Chapter 2 discussed as high modernist systems based on elections, bureaucracy and political parties. For Wolin, the US political system was not only unable to provide democracy, it was anti-democratic: embedding hierarchy, elitism and the concentration of power.[18] Opportunities for people to engage in public life, to develop democratic practices and to experience commonality and collective enjoyment, were diminished by modern politics. Hence, it cannot be assumed that the relation between the state and citizens is one of democratic engagement, participation, openness and accountability. State spaces are not given as places of and for democracy.[19] As a result, citizens must embrace new perspectives and places in order to make democratic experiences.

The shift from institutions to practices, from democracy as a form of government to an understanding of democracy as a mode of experience, comes with implications. If democracy shows itself mainly in terms of how it is practised and experienced, then its objects of interest are not ideational or abstract norms, values, preferences or (strategic) interactions. Rather, they are the routinized and material actions and tacit understandings of real people. Democratic practices are thus material practices reliant on bodies and artefacts.[20] This seems to be a truism, but most conventional accounts of democracy do without the materiality of people and things. Democratic practices are also anchored in and activate different forms of tacit knowledge. So, a shift from institutions to practices also means that we are more interested in what sort of (democratic) knowledge and meanings are expressed in these practices than in the sort of knowledge and meanings that institutions call their own and try to spread. Practices have a dual meaning. Based on tacit knowledge they are routine repetitions. At the same time, practices contain a structural openness due to their temporality.[21] An emphasis on practices as the nucleus of democracy implies that democracy can be different in different places and at different times, and that a great variety of democratic experiences and experiments can be made and witnessed when we refrain from seeing state institutions as the natural places to look for democracy. But still democracy needs a place: 'It's a paradox: while the democratic imagination is open and expansive, the practice has to be both bounded and grounded, embodied in particular populations and places. Only by taking root can democratic seeds spread.'[22]

According to Wolin, it is the task of citizens to create and reflect upon places of democratic engagement, action and experience. Activities of the citizenry should not be directed (only) to the state and the political structure the state predefines. Political and democratic action should be 'expressed not in one or two modes of activity – voting or protesting – but in many'.[23] Further, the emphasis on democratic practices expands the definition of citizenship. A citizen is not only, or even primarily, a bearer of rights and duties, but a political person whose life and actions are rooted in the places where their lives occur: 'Family, friends, church, neighbourhood, workplace, community, town, city. These relationships are the sources from which political beings draw power – symbolic, material, and psychological – and that enable them to act together.'[24]

The challenge for such an understanding of democracy is not to fall into the local trap or to be mistaken for a communitarian project trusting only in the unitary cultural experience of small-scaled communities. Two points need to be made clear: for one, the need to localize democratic practices is not due to the assumption that local practices are more democratic than practices at any other scale. Rather, it is due to the insight that material and tacit properties are always local in the sense that they take place in a specific locale at a specific time, and that only through these properties can practices be realized.

The other aspect at stake here is how practices relate the one to the many, the citizen to the community. Or, in more theoretical terms, how practices can fashion the demos. In the radical tradition of democracy, the demos cannot be assumed but is rather something that needs to be constituted and as such is never stable or complete. The constitution of the demos (or other collective identities) itself becomes part of democratic politics. This self-fashioning and re-fashioning of the demos is not an expert undertaking but the project of citizens and collectives, what Wolin calls 'craftspersons'; a craftsperson is someone 'who respects what he or she is working with – persons, relations, places, and needs – and knows the story of where they have come from'.[25] This is not an ideational or abstract endeavour but one based on bodily acts grounded in and acting upon places, temporalities and materialities. It is about people coming together in particular places at particular times to forge collective relations and goals. In other words, democracy needs to be grounded and, at the same time, generate its own (temporary) grounds.

Re-grounding democracy in the city

Democracy as material practice, constituting its own publics and places, resonates with much of the empirical work on urban democratic projects. How urbanites engage with urban space, and how they imagine what urban democracy should mean and look like, have changed in recent years. In many places urbanites are not satisfied with voting representatives to local governments or going to the ballots every now and then to voice preferences for this or that project. Even the fully-fledged participatory processes which were *le dernier cri* in the 1990s and early 2000s seem to have lost traction. All too often they are used to legitimize already established projects and decisions. In reaction, and as a claim for democracy, some urbanites across the world are trying to engage directly in the production of urban space. In this section, we try to make sense of this redirection of democracy against the backdrop of global urbanization. How can we relate material democratic practices to global forces of urbanization? And what is the place of the city in this? Can we still defend the city on democratic grounds?

For some time, the relation between the city and democracy was seen as self-evident. Cities as places of social encounters and proximity were a 'natural' location for democratic experience and experimentation. City life was the obvious basis for a vibrant public and the condition for political engagement within the structures of a pluralist democracy. Indeed, the 'city' has been important to the development of democracy, was crucial to classical theories of democracy, and has long been seen as a laboratory for political experimentation.[26] For some time, urban democracy meant in practice liberal democracy located in cities. The focus was on the same or similar institutions and politics as at the national level, but in a different and subordinated political jurisdiction, the city. However, this relationship between the city and democracy has been obscured by the dominance of the (nation) state in modern political theory and practice.[27] In our reimagining of an urban democracy, we take inspiration from the past, but our arguments are contingent on current conditions of global urbanization. It is not the reimagining of an idealized past of sovereign city-states or a nation-state democracy writ small.

As discussed in chapters 1 and 2, the seemingly self-evident relation between city and democracy has been undermined from both sides. The city as a hope for democracy has been questioned as cities have become more and more driven by global elites and their specific demands. Pluralism in cities has an increasingly strong upper-class accent, especially in the city centres. The transformation of the city is also due to processes of urbanization at the global scale. From this perspective the city itself turns into an ideology occluding our view of socio-spatial transformations.[28] Indeed, planetary urbanization demonstrates that the city as a social, spatial and political phenomenon has changed profoundly and can no longer be assumed as a stable and viable ground for democracy. However, if the city is no longer a coherent entity, the literature on planetary urbanization has yet to provide a means of reformulating the knotty relation between urban spaces, urbanity and democracy in the age of global urbanization.[29] Put differently, the debates on planetary urbanization have convincingly shown that the contemporary urban condition of the world cannot be grasped by conventional academic categories.[30] But it remains unclear if these spatial categories still provide meaning for democratic thought and action.

In this section, our argument is that the idea of the city – and not its traditional physical location, typical settlement structure or specific social configuration – still has purchase as an ever-present possibility and symbolic space for democratic action. However, we do not suggest that the city operates only as an imagined entity, or as an entrancing castle in the clouds. Rather, we follow Engin

Isin, who argues that the city, in contrast to the nation state, is a virtual *and* actual space:

> The actual city embodies things (building, roads, infrastructures, uses) as well as bodies within intrinsically related and proximate arrangements that constitute its physicality and materiality. The actual city is *urbs*. The city is also virtual in the sense that it is an association that exists beyond the actual bodies and things that constitute it. The virtual city is *civitas*.[31]

Whenever we use the term city, we usually imply both understandings. This makes the term so powerful because it foregrounds the relations between the physicality of buildings, of material infrastructures and the built environment, and the social arrangements, practices and meanings in a given place. The term 'city' links the visibility of place to the invisibility of all the norms, aspirations and demands co-constituting in this place. The city contains meanings, imaginaries and promises that are real and that exist beyond but not independently of the physicality of the actual city. But, as Isin insists, we should not conflate one with the other or reduce one to the other. The *urbs* does not generate *civitas* per se. Urbanized space does not inevitably become the city. It has to be reclaimed and lived as a city to become one. In turn, *civitas* needs actual spaces to become meaningful for urbanites. The social arrangements we connect with *civitas* and the city need to be brought down to the ground; they need to be materially inscribed.

So we understand Isin's argument as a plea to account for the materiality and the multiple, morphing sites of democratic engagement and citizenship. The term 'city' holds the political potential to do so in the context of global urbanization. The actual city is the place where acts of citizenship are performed, where people organize to self-govern on matters of public concern and where they confront the alienation and exploitation induced by urbanization – wherever this place is located on the map.[32]

The city is thus the place where democracy is practised and imagined. Hence, the city escapes the idea of contained political or geographical scales. To hold on to the city also forces us to take the actual material environment into consideration when we think about democracy as practice and about the situations and controversies around which urban democratic publics emerge.[33]

Judith Butler makes a similar point. In her discussion of Hannah Arendt's concept of a space of appearance she argues that this space rests on demanding conditions.[34] The space of appearance where citizens can make claims public and encounter each other as equals and as political subjects depends on material and spatial conditions. This is because all practices and collective acts are (also) bodily acts. The bodies that emerge as publics are in need of physical and material support; they need sites, places where they can gather and be visible. Institutional places such as parliaments, committee boards and so on provide and are dependent on different sources than streets, market places or collective housing projects. The actuality of these places shapes, to a certain extent, the intensity and openness of interactions, encounters and negotiations. Hence, collective action does not constitute a space on its own, but rests on material conditions. In turn, public assemblies, once they are present, visible and acting, have the potential to transform the material conditions in which they act.

Of course, the fact that democracy needs a site where it can take place is nothing new.[35] But, as stated earlier, in contemporary democratic theory and political science, the physical and material location is rarely addressed or accounted for. This abstraction of people from places is apparent in the almost complete absence of democratic rights to intervene in the world immediately around us, such as our homes, streets and neighbourhoods, which are, in turn, given over to the rightful running of the state and the market. This is a view of democracy which ultimately abstracts us from the self-government of spaces of our everyday lives.

Cities in a conventional understanding are bounded, dense and diverse places that provide more opportunities for collective political action than rural areas. This is probably the most established and pertinent way of making the case for the city as a 'political context' of, or source for, democratic action.[36] In cities, different people can come together and develop a sense of collectivity, mostly in view of their needs for consumption and social reproduction. The density and diversity of cities increase the probability that people with similar life experiences can get in touch with each other, or find common cause in terms of specific needs. Democracy in cities is, in this way of thinking, particular, with cities providing fertile ground for mobilizing collectives of diverse and unlikely political actors or establishing social movements, as we detailed in Chapter 1.

We certainly agree that the city understood in this way is still an important source of democratic action; however, we would insist that, due to global urbanization, these urban sources of democratic organizing have escaped the confines of the city proper. At the same time, urbanization also provides new political sources that are much more embedded in urban collective life. As James Holston and Arjun Appadurai have convincingly shown, urbanization alters the geographies and rationalities of governance in ways that enable or compel urbanites – often those marginalized or excluded – to seek and find new ways of claiming space, voice and citizenship.[37] The feminist critique of planetary urbanization points in a similar direction. Kate Derickson and others argue that to fully grasp the realities of urban collective life one needs to understand the dialectics of the everyday and the global processes of urbanization without creating totalized abstractions.[38] Urbanization is always situated and generates positioned knowledges and different forms of resistances; to comprehend what is happening we therefore need to account for minor theories and the view from the outside. Situated knowledges and divergent practices are often deeply embedded in and related to the infrastructures, materialities and everyday rhythms of global urban spaces where the state recedes from view or takes on hybrid and multiple forms. Hence, urbanization not only provides a source as a political context for collective organizing, but also alters the ways urbanites see and act politically, thus shifting the democratic horizon. Urban collective life provides actual democratic spaces understood as spaces of engagement and conflicts. This is a democracy of lived places rather than of abstract rights and rules.

Global urbanization, we contend, not only transforms the sites and sources of politics but also the stake. The city as an actual and virtual democratic space becomes the very stake of democratic action. The city as a stake is the urban common-wealth where a vast array of values 'created by past generations and current residents' is located and in use.[39] The democratic struggle for the city is always also a struggle not to be excluded from this common value or social property to which every urbanite is contributing. Margaret Kohn makes a compelling case that the city as a collective oeuvre and urban common-wealth can be 'mobilized against the hegemonic view that private property and the commodity form are the only natural, legitimate, and efficient way of relating people to places'.[40] Indeed, as we will show throughout this book, urbanites across the globe do exactly this in a variety of places and contexts.

In these struggles, urbanites, collectives and diverse urban organizations bring the claim for a right to the city to life. As Kohn has argued, that claim should not be interpreted as a judicial or legal right but as a political claim which serves the purpose of gaining access to the city while also laying the ground for, and fuelling experiences of, acts of citizenship and solidarity.[41] In these different moments and patterns of city-claiming and city-making, 'movements of insurgent urban citizenship' can be generated.[42] This urban form of citizenship is about striving to become a member in the actual city composed of different materialities, objects, infrastructures and political agents. In line with the radical democracy tradition, this political assemblage has no predefined form, substance or boundary. Rather, in this sense, the city is virtual, it is an idea. But it becomes actual when things, matters of public concern and bodies are made visible as people come together to self-fashion the demos.

An *urban* democracy is, then, always concerned with the urban as common property and with how the value of urbanity is accessible and distributed between urbanites. The distinctly urban character of democracy comes from the impossibility of defining or legally limiting who can participate in these struggles. Urbanization generates different 'communities of strangers'[43] who have to address and form themselves as political agents in their own right. They often do so through their attempts to find resonances within their urban environments, generating alliances and common concerns in relation to food, water, transportation and the like. We understand these efforts to find resonance, to align bodies, materials and spaces in common cause, as a claim for urban self-government.

So, to summarize, how do we understand the city in contemporary struggles for democracy? Returning to Isin, the city is both actual and virtual. The city is the political imaginary which stands for the re-grounding of democracy in urban space and its ambition to self-government in proximate socio-material processes (i.e. urbanization). The struggle for the city is the struggle for democracy: to access, enjoy and co-determine the common-wealth generated by urbanization. 'City' is then the name for all those spaces where urban publics emerge and act. As a virtual space, the city provides the symbolic horizon where different struggles come together and have actual effects. Isin makes a key point when he argues that 'virtual bodies [i.e. states, nations, empires] are assemblages that are kept together by practices organized around and grounded in the city'.[44] We can think of this as a call not to make binary distinctions between the virtual state and the actual city. Rather, the city might be the ground where the state aims to assert its sovereignty and power, and where urban democracy is always caught in the tension between this claim for sovereignty and the claim for self-rule and resonance.

Democracy, the state and the city

It is one of the most vexed questions for projects of urban democracy – what to do about the state? Seek to co-opt it for the purposes of your own democratic project by gaining governmental office? Cooperate with it, while hoping to retain independence? Confront it and force change through the power of social movements? Ignore it and transgress its laws? Combine a range of the above? A definitive answer is impossible to find in historical examples and academic discussions. The growing uncertainty about the state's role in society adds to the doubt. Longstanding debates in the social sciences have emphasized the increasingly fluid, networked and generative nature of policy-making, as well as the contingent role of the state in liberal democracies. As discussed in chapters 1 and 2, for decades now scholars have been telling us that the state is increasingly fragmented and contradictory, increasingly subservient to global economic interests, and increasingly (often willingly) unfit for purpose when it comes to fulfilling its social contract. As Wendy Brown has laid bare, the advance of neoliberal political rationality should be understood as an attack on the very idea of the demos 'with its vanquishing of *homo politicus* by *homo oeconomicus*, with its hostility towards politics, with its economization of the terms of liberal democracy, and with its displacement of liberal democratic legal values and public deliberation with governance and new management'.[45] Ultimately, Brown notes, neoliberal rationality has been extremely effective in identifying capitalism with democracy. The state has been fundamental to this, becoming an instrument, for example, of austerity urbanism, and transforming itself, markets and society through the privatization, liberalization and financialization of everyday life.[46] Brown is referring mainly to liberal democracies, but her arguments about the conditioning of politics by neoliberal political rationality are applicable across political systems.

However, the issue of the state runs deeper, going to the core of political theory. From a radical democracy perspective the state is an inherently ambiguous object to say the least. Indeed, radical democracy theories tell us that we need to ground democracy outside of the state. But, at the same time, the state cannot be ignored either by activists themselves or by academics trying to make sense of practised democracy. Kohn is valuable here in highlighting a democracy/state nexus which can be productive, even if it is always ambivalent, for urban democracy.[47] She acknowledges – in the case of public spaces and transit justice – the emancipatory potential of 'urban social movements and the self-rule of people outside of the state'.[48] At the same time, she points out that when the focus is on 'the interests and needs of the least advantaged ... it is hard to imagine how to address the deficit in transit infrastructure in a megacity without the redistributive and planning capacity of the state'.[49] We might, rightfully, distrust the state when democratization is at stake; but, in real world politics, it would seem naive to ignore the dormant or actual potential of the state to re-order urban space and resources in more democratic ways.

The state's sovereign power means it can do things other organizations cannot, like collect taxes, provide public goods, make binding decisions and address the externalities of societal activities. The very form modern democracy has come to take – representative, electoral – is a realignment of the original idea of an assembled demos in relation to the large scale and complexity of the nation state. The spread of democracy in nineteenth-century Europe came to be organized predominantly around the institutional frameworks and imaginaries of the nation state. The liberal democracies that took shape in this period were from the start 'saturated with capitalist powers and values'.[50] Despite the gains made in terms of representative democracy since, state institutions and legal regimes have, as Wolin argued, also secured the privileges of the elite, private property and capital regimes, and embedded racial, gender and other social inequalities. The state has been at the centre of the forces which make us unfree, that contain, divide and subdue the demos in its very name.[51]

As Brown has stated, there is a 'deep argument' about what democracy entails, and both a 'long historical shadow and a contemporary struggle are also in play'.[52] The notion of the democracy/state nexus reveals the two competing pulls that have framed democratic politics – collective self-rule (demos) confronting the desire and capacity for order (state). For a democratic project to persist, to gain traction, it will have to engage, again and again, with the main institution of political rule – the state. Indeed, this is the perceived function of the state in conventional understandings of democracy: to rule, to prevail. The democracy/state nexus has to be navigated because, quite simply, it cannot be avoided. But how are we to deal with this tension between democracy and the state?

We might start with the idea of locating democratic projects at – contingent – distances to the state. The notion of a distance to the state has been evoked by urban scholars like Swyngedouw, drawing on the work of radical democracy theorists like Michael Abensour.[53] It taps into the core theoretical idea that democracy can never be contained within the state, indeed must often be its enemy. The state is quite simply on the wrong side of many struggles, including in nominal democracies. Locating democracy at a distance to the state appears to make sense. But questions abound.

What does 'distance' denote? Simply standing apart from the state? Is democratic politics, in essence, always outside of the state? Or is some form of engagement with the state foreseen? If so, how should we think about distance in both practical and theoretical terms?

Simon Critchley provides a convincing way of dealing with these questions. He too begins with the deep paradox for democracy presented by the state: the impossibility of democracy being provided for or located within the state, paralleled by the infeasibility of fully avoiding the state's reach in contemporary societies.[54] He offers us a normative-theoretical argument against the state and a political-strategic way of placing the state in relation to democracy. Taking inspiration from Marx, Critchley argues that a democratic politics arises from people freely associating, organizing, and developing places and practices of collective rule, locally, situationally.[55] Democratic politics is also fundamentally about driving the deformation of the state as a political force. Hence, politics is about establishing a 'distance' to the state to allow political projects to take shape. The distance is not only necessary, it is democratic in that it provides the very conditions in which 'true democracy' can emerge. However, this distance is interstitial, internal to the state. By this Critchley means that it is impossible to escape the state's social-spatial reach – articulating distance will always mean adopting positions within and upon the state's space.[56] This lack of external distance to the state is also one of imagination as well as power – democratic politics is about opening up possibilities from within, but aiming beyond the status quo (and the state). Ultimately, Critchley is arguing that, such is the reach of the modern state, in our minds as well as in laws and institutions, political projects can never truly escape the state. Democratic politics remains tied in this tension with the state. To take his argument an iteration further, there can be no true democratic space beyond the state.[57]

Urban democratic practices, publics and places

This chapter has engaged with the concept of democracy to try to understand and interpret the political action we observe around the globe. We have argued that in the face of global urbanization there is a need to reformulate what democracy means, and to address key questions afresh: How should democracy be practised or claimed? And where might we find it? In our attempt to make sense of the shifting ground of urban democracy, we first traced visions of radical democracy. Second, we discussed the implications of ongoing socio-spatial transformations for how and where democracy can be enacted and located. This was related to the question of the city as an idea and category of practices. Finally, we reflected upon the relation between democracy and the state and the need to formulate interstitial distances of irresolvable tension. In this final section we outline ways of reimagining urban democracy not as a model but as a way to situate and proliferate democratic possibilities.

Our interpretation of democracy takes its cues from traditions of radical democracy theory, following Wolin's work in particular. Democracy can never be settled as a form or institutional arrangement. It gets its vibrancy from the urge to always democratize democracy as a form of politics conducted through the ongoing forging of publics and collective experiences. From this perspective, democracy can literally happen or be realized everywhere, from street corners to parliaments, from city squares to ordinary infrastructure networks, from workplaces to the core of the administrative state. Radical democratic theory helps us to make a conceptual shift in how we look at current political struggles and more mundane practices in urban areas. Indeed, it is often only through this perspective that we recognize the democratic quality of these practices.

We suggest three empirical moves away from the more dominant stance of state-based democracy, moves which will guide our discussions in the chapters to come. First, the emergent urban democracy we envision might best be approached through its distinct practices rather than its institutional forms. We are so used to taking institutions as entry points for the study of democracy that it is easy to assume they gave birth to democratic politics and are the solid basis for its continuation, rather than being the outcome of democratic struggles and the subject of constant contest and shaping. Democratic and democratizing practices give meaning to the idea and the institutions of democracy, rather than the other way round.

Second, urban democracy is better understood through its entanglement with urban places and materialities instead of in terms of its jurisdictional scale. The concept of scale is deeply enshrined in a state-centred understanding of politics and democracy. Scale is often equated with political level or jurisdiction, and does not really engage with place-based spatial or material realities. But what is distinctive about an *urban* democracy is exactly the relational materiality, the complex web of human and non-human agents and environments, that makes up a place and conditions how urbanites engage therein. So, we do not suggest a shift to the local scale, but rather an engagement with places and locales where practices of and for democracy emerge.

Third, and in contrast to statist visions, democracy does not start with an empirically and legally given political subject of a demos. As will be argued in Chapter 5 especially, political subjects in an urban democracy are not delineated and confined by legal statuses or the idea of a culturally and spatially bounded community. Political subjects are emergent. Through urban democratic publics, matters of concern become visible and at the same time these publics provide the grounds for different political subjectivities.

This shift in perspective points to a problem with how we approach the question of democracy. For the radical democracy tradition, democracy escapes the settled institutional forms and terms we are so used to using and referring to. A new vocabulary is required to grasp how the city can transform democracy. It must start from the idea that democracy exists in the forging of common causes and the organization of society according to principles of collective self-rule. Bringing this idea into relation with the city, the general aim of struggles for democracy, as we have said, is to access, enjoy and co-determine the urban common-wealth. The urban is understood as the common good, a form of social property created by all. The value that comes from urbanity and from urbanizing spaces should be shared among all urbanites. Most struggles centre on this issue because the fruits of urbanity are often extracted through the legal instrument of private property. In and through these struggles a community of strangers can emerge as an urban public and claim citizenship. Various acts of urban citizenship and a proliferation of different urban publics are visible in these struggles. Most often they do not address the state or state agencies but articulate the aim for self-government in relation to the urban environment around them.

Our turn to the radical strand of democratic thinking is motivated by the need to locate the politics of producing urban spaces in the here and now, as Chapter 2 argued. As such, urban democracy is concerned neither with revolution as 'event' nor with reform as process, but with the proliferation of practices, places and publics of democratic self-government. Urban collective life acts as the setting but also the object of these projects as they attempt to reveal and challenge the dominating forces of urbanization. Around the globe we can observe attempts by urbanites and urban collectives to access, participate in and co-determine the production of urban space. These are often bodily and purposive practices embedded in urban collective life, directed towards socio-material environments and their transformation. Looking through these democratic practices, we see that their impact is really in articulating democratic publics. In this sense, the localness of these practices is not so much directed towards a specific scale of social-political organization and governance as towards locating democratic action in and through space. There is, therefore, an immediate relation between the claims and issues at stake and the places where these claims are made. Calling the streets or the squats democratic spaces is not to say that they are privileged or somehow intrinsic scales for organizing democracy, but rather that they can be generative of democratic places. These democratic places can be situated or supported by state institutions usually identified as democratic, but they are not restricted to them. In fact, new or emergent democratic spaces might alter or challenge existing state spaces.

In the chapters that follow, the book takes a more empirical turn and examines often overlooked practices, publics and places in order to make sense of and relocate the city as a democratic idea. In doing so, we reveal the knowledge, ambition and work entailed in democratic projects as well as their contingent outcomes.

4

Self-governing Urbanization

As detailed in the previous chapters, an urban reimagining of democracy centres on the ethos of self-government. On the most basic level, urban self-government means that those who co-produce urban spaces should also govern those places. Rather than exploitation and domination through urbanization – the target of various often competing capital- and/or state-led urban development strategies – the aim is to nurture situated and common practices of producing, contesting and enjoying urban space. Self-government in this view is a way of making and sharing political experience and democratic knowledge. It encourages the articulation of shared concerns and political engagement around those concerns.

But it is more than this. As we argue throughout the book, the striving for urban self-government brings struggles and meaning to life, embedding claims for an urban democracy in the everyday fabric.[1] Self-government is both a reaction to urbanization, in the way it re-localizes politics, and part of urbanization, shaping its spatial and political conditions. Urban self-government does, then, entail practices of locating democratic politics and producing urban spaces to negotiate and establish communality in the here and now. It is, in part, always a process of relating to and resonating with the spatial transformations, big and small, within urbanization and establishing alternative modes of collective governing. This form of democracy is about spatial practices, embedded in and directed towards urban spaces and territories. Indeed, if we understand urban space as the common property of its inhabitants, then it is crucial to examine how urbanites are actually inhabiting it and how they can shape their modes of inhabitation.

The scope for participating in and shaping the urban spaces in which one lives and interacts with others can be depressingly narrow – even in political systems where democratic self-government is formally assured. An example from Switzerland is telling in this regard. Juch-Areal is an area on the periphery of Zurich, jammed between a motorway to the north and rail tracks to the south, both connecting Zurich to the rest of Switzerland. The area around the adjoining station, Zurich-Altstetten, has recently been developed into a complex of offices, hotels and apartments. While writing this chapter, the last of the wooden huts or shanties that had covered the Juch-Areal site were demolished, and construction is underway for the new ZSC Lions ice hockey stadium designed by the renowned architects Caruso St John. Prior to that the local police had evicted around fifty squatters from three shanties on the Juch-Areal. Shortly before they were removed by the police, the squatters compiled a booklet entitled 'Humans in Shanties' (*Menschen in Baracken*).[2] The stories detailed therein are indicative of both the lived experience of urbanization as a form of domination and the striving for a democratization of urbanization through collective self-government.

The Juch-Areal, owned by the city of Zurich, first became of interest to local construction companies in the early 1960s. At that time, the economy was booming and the city was experiencing hitherto unseen growth. This was made possible by the availability of underpaid and disenfranchised labour from southern European countries, mainly Italy and Spain. Their subordination to urbanization was inherent to development in the Zurich area. When the construction companies cast their eye on the Juch-Areal they were looking, like many other companies, for somewhere to house their seasonal migrant workers. While the federal state pursued a laissez-faire policy in relation to migrant workers, it was nevertheless necessary for the companies to register a place of residency for their workers in order to obtain work permits. This gave rise to numerous exploitative practices, whereby seasonal migrant workers were housed in derelict buildings or shanties and containers. The construction of shanties was widespread, as were the frequent fires that took numerous lives as well as the few possessions the migrant workers had. Not much is known about everyday life on the Juch-Areal in Zurich in the 1960s and onwards. At that time, the site was located at the fringe of the city, surrounded by traffic infrastructure and industrial and commercial buildings. There were no social amenities or public facilities. It is hard to imagine that these barracks ever became a proper home, remaining little more than a place to sleep between the hours of hard work. There is evidence that workers organized and fought back against the exploitation of their labour power and the violation of their human dignity. However, they were quickly confronted by the police and threatened with deportation.

In the last twenty years of its existence, the Juch-Areal served as a centre for asylum seekers. It was enclosed by a fence and subject to strict regulations. The people who lived there usually were not granted asylum in Switzerland. They were forced to stay in these shacks until their deportation to the countries they had fled. This could take only a few days or as long as half a year. In any case, the asylum seekers at the Juch-Areal were deprived of all political, social and economic rights except those of eating, sleeping and waiting.

The Juch-Areal case is useful in illustrating what urban democracy might entail, if only because of the completeness of its absence: residents without political citizenship; urbanites with no control or say over their lives or the spaces they inhabit; urbanization driving their exploitation; profit logics determining the fate of people and places; political power located apart from everyday life, the reserve of the state and big business. From this example we might conclude that urbanization creates only challenges for democracy, in its disruptions, its movement of people from one place to another, its deepening of capital interests and its potent urge to transform urban places. In recent decades, much of the research in the field of urban politics and metropolitan governance has indeed been devoted to the question of finding the 'right' political scale at which to address the challenges of urbanization. The general thinking was that there must be a solution at hand within existing institutional frameworks, which just needed to be adapted to global urban processes. Magnusson, however, turned this question on its head: 'Our problem is not to rescale our political units, but rather to invent a politics appropriate to a de-territorialized existence.'[3] He suggested that local self-government might provide such a politics. We adapt this idea by hinging it more directly to urbanization and the production of urban space.

In this chapter we take housing and property regimes as a prism through which to depict the spectrum of relations between urbanization and self-government, drawing contrasts with the state logic of democracy (or state-centred democracy). We start by arguing that democracy can begin at home, or, in more conceptual terms, that the home can be a space and infrastructure for self-government and solidarity within urbanization, even in a context where property rights and markets appear to dominate. The overall purpose of the chapter is to throw some light on the rich, relational and multifaceted array of urban self-government strategies practised or strived for in urban areas. We refer to a diversity of places (Barcelona, Berlin, Los Angeles, Zurich) and identify a range of locally specific political strategies for urban self-government. We conclude the chapter by discussing the ambivalent possibilities of self-government.

Home as a gateway to urban democracy

In everyday language, when someone refers to their *home* or to home in general, they usually mean more than just a place to sleep and live. Home is not just a physical place, a location where one lives. It is also a site of social reproduction, connected to feelings of belonging, aspiration, memories and community. Thus, home is a significant space, a 'spatial imaginary'[4] that connects feelings and experiences to a certain context, helps us locate ourselves in the world, and provides a place through which we can relate to the world. Yet, home is not a safe place for everyone. Feminist scholars have made this point for a while, but it became obvious to ever more people during the Covid-19 pandemic as a result of the quarantine orders introduced in most countries.[5] Nevertheless, home, and more importantly the struggle for a decent place to live, can also be crucial to forging political solidarities and alternatives.[6] Crucially, home is not a given, as the various forms of housing crisis around the world make painfully clear. Most people living in cities are not in a position to freely determine the nature of their home.[7] Rather, they are dependent on existing housing opportunities and the wider socio-economic relations in which they are embedded. From the struggles around informal housing to a lack of access to basic shelter, through ballooning rental prices devouring low and middle incomes, housing lays bare the socio-economic injustices produced by the commodification of global urban life.

This tension between the immediate need for shelter and the desire for a proper home on the one hand, and the distant and often impenetrable housing markets on the other, spurs political struggles across the globe, fuelled by aspirations for self-government. Hence, the spatial imaginary of 'home' is not just about stability and finding an habitual mode of living. It is also about contesting the housing situation by producing ruptures and differences.[8] These can be organized collectively or they can reside in the mundane things we decide to do differently, the moves that disrupt the normal rhythms and repetitions of the everyday.

The Covid-19 pandemic was telling in this regard. With its stay-at-home and quarantine imperatives the policy response to the pandemic has exacerbated the already tense post-2008 global housing crisis. The pandemic confirmed the great importance of housing in multiple ways, exposing the market and state logics which deny the use-value of housing as shelter, a safe place and a node for collective engagements of support. In this context, several initiatives emerged to protect tenants from evictions and to house the unhoused. While well intentioned, and often with concrete benefits, such projects ultimately work to perpetuate the financialization of housing, so pivotal to the crisis in the first place, through continuing to see homes as a commodity.[9] Housing for many has long been disconnected from its social functions and the meanings of dwelling.[10] The financial crisis heightened this, underscoring the powerlessness of many to shape the spaces they inhabit and have a claim to. It is exactly these qualities that we should insist upon in any project of democracy. As Michele Lancione states, the claim for decent housing is also 'about finding ways to enable what home can do for people in the widest possible sense'.[11]

In Europe, the United States and many countries of the global south, housing struggles have been fought and are still being fought in governmental arenas and state-centred institutions. From the late nineteenth century onwards, and due to rapid industrial urbanization, housing has been a contested issue. Political organizations of different orientations articulated housing as an issue of public concern and demanded political action by governmental agencies at various levels. As a result, many countries witnessed a huge expansion of public housing as part of the post-Second World War reconstruction and the wider modernist, welfarist renewal of towns and cities. The interventionist state edging out the market and creating space for less commodified forms of housing and social life was crucial, and made a life-changing difference to many people's lives, even if there were well-documented problems of discrimination against, and displacement of, low income and ethnic groups within many of the projects implemented. In any case, in this period, the 'public' in public housing was by and large synonymous with the state, which itself was a provider of basic welfare.[12]

Often, however, the state plays an ambiguous role in housing markets due to its entanglement with existing property regimes, which aggravate the tensions between the desire for a home and the impenetrability of the housing system. One cannot look at the (unfulfilled) aspirations of urban self-government without considering urban property regimes.[13] Ananya Roy has noted that the property regime of possessive individualism, so commonplace in Europe and the United States, rests ultimately on state enforcement. This invokes a paradox, namely 'that if possessive individualism as an ontological claim to freedom rests on the tenet of property, then property itself depends on state power'.[14] In a similar vein, Daniel Loick used squatting to demonstrate how the idea and practice of property is deeply entangled with the idea of sovereignty. Property regimes, he argues, are a dispositive of power arranging and reshuffling social and political arrangements.[15] Such regimes do not, as is generally assumed in liberal political theory, enable the use of goods and resources but rather impede the use of urban resources and spaces. Property is exclusive and alienating as it prevents people from relating in meaningful ways with their urban surroundings. In response, Loick proposes that we should all have the right *not* to be included in regimes of property. This is what he calls the squatting solution. Making use of a building without appropriating it can be a non-sovereign way of being political and of self-governing. Squatting can open up new relationships between citizens and state around housing. If, for instance, the state forgoes its role as the enforcer of property rights, becoming instead the facilitator of urban collective life, then the dominant apparatus of property would no longer hold. This opens up an opportunity for citizens to rearrange or transgress existing property regimes.[16]

We understand *housing as a gateway*[17] to wider struggles for urban self-government. It can act as a material political infrastructure around which collectives are forged. The point here is that housing should be considered a field of democratic politics, in which citizens are foregrounded, rather than a field of rotating competition and cooperation between state and market, or public and individual interests, logics and agents. It can and should be a field in which the potential for self-government is expanded. The following sections discuss examples that show how homes can become both places where self-government is practised and an infrastructure through which it proliferates across urban space.

Home as a space and infrastructure

The friction between the needs, aspirations and hopes of people for a home and the often cruel reality of the housing system is a shared feature of most struggles for decent housing. The despair and frustration at not being able to find or keep a home is often overwhelming.[18] It is also not self-evident that people will find the energy and courage to come together and organize against the array of power structures confronting them. But they frequently have, and often in diverse ways. For instance, squatters all over the world repeatedly remind us of the politically disruptive and socially productive quality of taking over vacant urban space, of alternative home-making, and of the continuing appeal of self-governing urban spaces. Vasudevan understands squatting as one of many occupation-based practices emergent around the globe that seek to materialize an alternative social order.[19] Through squatting, urbanites relate in different, complex and performative ways to processes of home-making and the resources cities provide. They are motivated by the desire (or demand) to participate in the production of urban space. Reclaiming space in this way is often a transformative project based on collaboration and co-production outside formal politics. These practices do not appeal to abstract or distant arenas of decision-making. They enact, in an immediate and bodily fashion, what they strive for.

One of the biggest squats that Switzerland has ever seen, the Wohlgroth Squat, which lasted from 1991 to 1993, might serve as an illustration. It was an experiment in the democratization of space and the built environment – of co-living, dwelling and solidarity. In a book published shortly after the squat was evicted, the squatters looked back: 'Our claim for an autonomous culture is not just a claim for musical concerts and beer. Rather, we insist on spaces of self-determination, open living space, where we can live together holistically and according to our own ideas ... The prohibition of our way of life is a prohibition of ourselves.'[20] The accounts of the squatters give life to the idea of home/dwelling as self-rule, an idea motivated and driven by the desire to co-assemble, co-maintain and co-produce urban spaces. It is also an attempt to overcome exclusion and alienation through a politicization of urban everyday practices. To return to Simone and Pieterse's concept, it seeks to facilitate *resonance* in urban collective life, through the alignment of people, materials and space.[21]

Struggling for a home is thus more than an attempt to fulfil private choices; rather, it is a way to relate oneself as a person or a collective to the wider socio-material world. It can be a means to overcome the power relations inscribed in the materiality and sociability of the city and to (re-)establish a form of connection and resonance with the environment. It is both a way to become political in relation to urbanization and a mode of locating politics, building the spaces and infrastructures of self-government.

Among the many examples discussed in the recent academic literature, one of the most striking and well known is the story of the Platform for Mortgage-Affected People (PAH) in Barcelona, which demonstrates how the fight for a home can turn into a wider urban political struggle. The history of the PAH goes back to the beginning of Spain's economic crisis in 2008, as jobs were lost and the notion of a democracy through home-ownership collapsed.[22] The first assembly of the PAH took place in February 2009 and the prime goal was 'to generate a space of confidence, where people lose their fear, empower themselves and verify that alone they cannot but together they can'.[23] In the following years, the PAH was able to politicize housing to the extent that people threatened by evictions were not ashamed or fearful and instead started to challenge the political foundations on which the housing system was built. This meant thinking anew about housing markets, property rights, ownership and the role of the state in promoting and maintaining these political-institutional arrangements. Through the PAH assembly meetings and the collective practices of physically blocking evictions with human shields, solidarities and new understandings of rights to housing and urban spaces were established.

Through the actions of the PAH, activists started to relate in new and collective ways to the socio-spatial transformations they witnessed. The PAH thus enabled the emergence of the kind of practices and consciousness identified by political theorists like Wolin as vital to democracy: that of ordinary citizens realizing their political potential through the development of common concerns and decision-making.[24] The PAH was also successful in generating a wider project for urban democracy, eventually leading to the capture of Barcelona's local government through the central role played by the PAH in the citizen platform Barcelona en Comú.[25] The PAH is therefore not only an example of how the need for shelter and the desire for a home led to a struggle against an opaque and hostile housing market supported by the sovereign power of the state. It also reveals the potential of such struggles to generate momentum, to take on wider political meanings and to engage with the fundamentals of how urban spaces, like those of housing, are produced. The PAH went beyond protesting against the state or aiming for state power by developing new ways to situate politics in Barcelona, turning the housing crisis into a platform for thinking about housing politics and the political means that should be used to transform the city more generally.

The story of the PAH and the new municipalist model of Barcelona has gained widespread attention amongst urban scholars and activists. But there are also less well known, perhaps more mundane cases where, for instance, housing struggles and the building of homes not only help to forge collectives but the homes themselves serve as infrastructures of political contention and self-rule. Leandro Minuchin details two examples from Rosario (Argentina) and Guayaquil (Ecuador) which are illustrative of similar stories all over the world.[26] He speaks of a material politics of construction which stands for a different way of being political, one based on immediate action upon urban space. Minuchin vividly depicts how participation in the construction process, the self-building of homes, can be seen as a way of producing and using urban infrastructures for democratic purposes. These infrastructures are used as material mediums to disrupt the embedded and often alienating institutional arrangements of urbanization, such as massive state-led but market-oriented housing development projects. The physical process of collectively building homes, community schools or other common facilities is a way of translating dispersed, perhaps even inconsistent, insurgent ideas into the visible material world. Socio-material infrastructures of self-government emerge, everyday routines are re-coded, and imaginaries of urbanization as a localized self-governing process take shape.[27]

Strategies for urban self-government

As we argued above, political struggles around housing are rarely just about the exchange value of homes but assert different ways of engaging with the world. To be transformative, housing struggles have to engage strategically with property regimes, the state, market actors and policy discourse. Projects will have to be astute, working across scales and spaces, building from the home (and its multiple meanings) into wider processes of urbanization. There are many examples of self-government in urban housing, especially when we look at squatting. However, squatting is frequently a temporary mode of dwelling and more often than not a rather marginal mode of urban living; its original acts of transgression and communal living are unlikely to be followed by all. Like oases in urban deserts, squats remind us of what might be possible, but they themselves cannot turn the desert into something else.[28] As instructive as cases like the Wohlgroth Squat are, a plea for urban self-government centred on the home needs to encompass a broader set of political strategies if it is to carry the potential to generate support and expand through diverse urban areas. There will thus not be one single or even pure form of collective self-government, but contingent and recurring attempts to advance it.

When we look for wider and more permanent struggles and forms of self-government in housing, we find diverse attempts in different places and times. Some maintain a kind of insular existence, others confront the local state as a terrain of self-government, and some aim for broader political organization, with housing more clearly positioned as a gateway for a democratization of urbanization. We now discuss examples of these strategies of self-government, returning, first, to Zurich before moving on to Berlin and Los Angeles. The cases are described in relation to their political contexts, and not presented as ideal types but as productive and contingent examples of expanding self-government and democratic potential. All share the idea of transcending housing markets based on possessive individualism, but they differ to some extent in terms of the practices they adopt and, more substantively, their stance towards the local state.

Zurich: reinventing housing cooperatives as a resource of urban self-government

The case of Zurich is illustrative because it shows how an established 'tool' of housing policy, not-for-profit housing cooperatives, can be reinvented as a resource for more transformative purposes.[29] In 1995, a few years after the Wohlgroth Squat was cleared, the Oerlikon Bührle Immobilien AG offered a different site to another urban collective, Kraftwerk 1. To be clear, this was not a benevolent move but a strictly economic decision. With Zurich enduring a severe economic recession, Oerlikon Bührle Immobilien AG faced numerous stalled office construction projects and was thus sitting on many undeveloped real estate plots. Kraftwerk 1, today an established and still politically progressive housing cooperative, emerged then as a collaboration between different urban political organizations. At the beginning, it was arguably more of a theoretically informed project than, say, the Wohlgroth Squat. It sought to build on the cultural and political openings that squats provided in the city. In 1993, a group of people assembled around the Konzeptgruppe Städtebau (urban design concept group) and the Ssenter for Applied Urbanism (SAU)[30] published the book *Kraftwerk 1*,[31] in which the authors presented a vision for housing in a deindustrializing city. Following the publication, a series of workshops and gatherings were held and the decision was made to found the housing cooperative Kraftwerk 1. The construction of a residential building on the site offered by Oerlikon Bührle Immobilien AG took place between 1998 and 2001. As a founding member recalls, the decision to form a cooperative was contested and far from obvious, because 'for us housing cooperatives were the organizational form of "the others" [*die Anderen*]'.[32]

This reference to 'the others' needs some explaining. In Zurich, housing cooperatives (i.e. not-for-profit housing providers) have a long and successful history in building affordable and community-oriented housing. Established in the late nineteenth century, housing cooperatives became instrumental in the local state's strategy to provide affordable housing in the early twentieth century. Additionally, the cooperatives were part of an attempt to placate the labour movement and those demanding more radical change in housing policy (such as socializing land or imposing stricter regulations on rents). In this period, one in three apartments in Zurich was built by housing cooperatives. While the cooperatives were never incorporated into the machinery of the local public administration, the influence of local government on their operation and strategy was nonetheless significant.

In the second half of the twentieth century, however, the close ties to the local state caused the depoliticization of housing cooperatives. Most became settled institutions, focused on their existing housing stock and residents. What began as a movement of progressive organizations aiming for the common good increasingly became an exclusive club-like phenomenon, associated with relatively conservative values centred on family and community. The goal of most cooperatives was to provide decent homes for 'average' (i.e. non-divorced, male-breadwinner) Swiss families. Non-Swiss residents but also single mothers/fathers or communal living groups were often excluded.

This was plain to see in the composition of residents in the cooperatives. In the 1970s only 4 per cent of them were non-Swiss citizens, compared to 16 per cent of all households in Zurich. Over the last twenty years, however, this gap has become smaller due to the more inclusive visions and practices called for by the new, more politicized housing cooperatives. So, when the member of Kraftwerk 1 describes housing cooperatives as 'the others', this refers specifically to the period of the 1980s and 1990s, when Swiss middle-class lifestyles dominated, the atmosphere was 'petty bourgeois and musty', and you could find numerous 'No Trespassing' signs in the backyards.[33]

Kraftwerk 1, along with similar cooperatives, inaugurated a period of rejuvenation. Housing cooperatives were established to experiment with different forms of urban living.[34] They were driven by a far more ambitious vision of the social and political purposes to which such cooperatives could be put. The development of these cooperatives was no doubt greatly helped by the already favourable conditions in the city. There were well-established legal principles, means of financial support, and political legitimacy for non-profit housing forms such as collective property, democratic management and the decommodification of homes. Housing cooperatives are not permitted to make a profit from rents or to offer apartments for sale. Within this framework, the new cooperatives implemented structures of self-rule, participation and co-production. The measures went well beyond the standard of many cooperatives, with private apartments supplemented by common inside and outside spaces. Shortly after the completion of the Kraftwerk 1 building, a founding member, Andreas Hofer, confided that 'the realization of the Kraftwerk changed my view of the city. Rather than seeing the city from the perspective of one who is a victim of it, I perceive it as shapeable.'[35]

But the building of Kraftwerk 1 was not without its ambiguities. For some, the urban utopia turned into a murky reality as the housing cooperative signed the contract with the Oerlikon Bührle Immobilien AG, renowned for its arms trade with Nazi Germany and other authoritarian regimes. Furthermore, some crucial ideas, such as communal living in diversity, proved to be more difficult to achieve than expected. The first residents of Kraftwerk were more homogeneous than had been hoped for. In contrast to the city average, they were predominantly Swiss and had higher education degrees. However, following the creation of a solidarity fund and cooperation with existing social institutions, it was possible to make Kraftwerk 1 more accessible to a broader population. The cooperative has since constructed two other residential buildings on the outskirts of the city. Currently, Kraftwerk 1 collaborates with Allgemeine Baugenossenschaft Zürich (ABZ) and the city of Zurich in the development of the Koch-Areal, the last big squat in the city, occupied since 2013 by more than 100 squatters.

Berlin: remunicipalization for the urban society

The Berlin case we explore is a little different as self-government here is articulated in direct relation to the local state. The aim of the housing remunicipalization movement is not simply to bring the housing stock back under the control of the state, but to reposition and repurpose the state in relation to 'urban society' in the form of a public-commons partnership.[36] It is, then, a project enacting urban society and reframing the state in relation to it. From the mid-1990s to 2007, the state of Berlin sold large parts of its housing stock to the private sector, reducing state-owned housing units by more than 40 per cent. This was part of a wider programme of privatization and budgetary cuts in response to increasing local state indebtedness, which itself was driven by the costs of reunifying the city after the Cold War division, economic decline and governmental mismanagement and corruption.[37] Alongside the sale of housing stock, the state abandoned supply-side subsidies, weakening not-for-profit housing cooperatives and attracting capital-rich developers. Market logics were further embedded in 2000, when the city's government (Der Senat von Berlin) established a professional entity to manage public property and housing units outside the core public administration – the Liegenschaftsfond Berlin GmbH & Co. KG. The Liegenschaftsfond turned the public housing stock into an asset to be utilized by the government for different (and commercial) purposes.[38] The result was the increased commodification of the housing market in Berlin and its spatially uneven development, as public stock became private throughout the city, alongside a profound restructuring of Berlin as a whole.[39] As the German economy in general, and the Berlin economy in particular, grew from the mid-2000s onwards, this has translated into steep increases in rents.

The transformation of housing policy in Berlin has been contested by various urban movements and resident groups.[40] In 2018, a broad coalition of housing activists formulated a citizen's initiative or petition (Volksbegehren: Deutsche Wohnen & CO Enteigen), which in September 2021 was successful in securing the backing of enough residents in Berlin to force the city government to enact a law enabling the state to remunicipalize the housing stock of large real estate companies. More precisely, the initiative demands that private real estate companies who own more than 3,000 housing units should be expropriated and their housing stock transferred to common property (*Gemeineigentum*). Compensation for this transfer should be well below market price, and the communalized housing stock should then be administered by a not-for-profit public law institution with the participation of Berlin residents.[41]

The current struggle against Berlin's housing policy is not just about advancing a more active role for the local state, using government institutions and policy to edge big business out of housing. It represents a much more substantive struggle for greater self-government. The coalition advancing the initiative is broad and encompasses many of the social groupings that Margit Mayer has identified as specific to contemporary urban movements: radical autonomous groups, middle-class urbanites, disparate groups sharing a precarious existence, and those who feel marginalized and excluded.[42]

The campaign seeks to by-pass representative politics through the use of an instrument of direct democracy to change housing policy. Resort to a citizens' petition is indicative of a scepticism towards established formal institutions of political representation, even in a context where nominally progressive parties – the Left (Die Linke), the Greens (Bündnis 90/Die Grünen) and the Social Democratic Party of Germany (Sozialdemokratische Partei Deutschlands) – are in coalition government (2016–). While the demand to socialize housing seems at first glance to be a sign of trust in the state, a closer look reveals this not to be the case. The petition makes it clear that the expropriation should be pursued in the name of 'urban society' and not in the name of the state. The resolution uses the terms 'socialization' (*Vergesellschaftung*) and 'remunicipalization' (*Rekommunalisierung*), and does not refer to a direct return to the state (*Verstaatlichung*).

It is therefore not just another demand directed towards the state as such, but addresses the municipality and urban society as political authorities distinct from though interwoven with the state. In their resolution of 25 October 2018, for a law on the socialization of land (Beschluss für ein Vergesellschaftungsgesetz von Grund und Boden), the coalition behind the initiative states that in the governing board of the to-be-formed public institution, tenants, employees and 'representatives of the urban society ... regardless of their status of citizenship' should hold the majority over representatives of the city's executive. The goal of the initiative is not solely to start a process of decommodification of the existing housing stock, but also to kickstart a process of democratizing the governance of vital urban resources. The expansion of collective self-rule is brought into relation with the question of what the state can do for democratic projects (a point to which we return in more detail in Chapter 6).

Los Angeles: confronting the local state with self-government

The examples from Los Angeles are different to the two discussed above as they emerge in a context where possessive individualism in housing is more deeply established and the political-legal system is less likely to give in to pressure for more collective approaches. Unlike in Zurich, there are no political-legal conditions conducive to developing housing cooperatives. Unlike in Berlin, the notion of public housing is not a recent memory. The strategy and modality of urban self-government in Los Angeles is therefore much more adversarial than in Zurich or Berlin, with much more emphasis on creating oppositional stances and identities. The urban growth coalition for which Los Angeles has become famous, or infamous, relies to a great extent on the conviction that the urban landscape can be drawn and redrawn as desired. In contrast to the two European cities discussed above, the city government has allied itself to business interests and growth at least since the late 1950s – albeit with some signs of decline since the late 1990s. The expansion of opportunities for minorities or vulnerable populations was never a policy goal. Rather, urban development projects were often used for displacement and aggressive gentrification.[43]

In the domain of housing there was a short period of public housing investment in the 1940s and early 1950s. As Don Parson has detailed, through these projects 'one might glimpse the Left's vision of a modern Los Angeles'.[44] With the Cold War politics of the Red Scare taking hold in the 1950s, the Left was eliminated from formal politics and the efforts to build a more just Los Angeles through public housing were extinguished. A pro-growth coalition gained dominance, encompassing members of the Democratic Party, the Republican Party and organized labour. Those who did not support this political direction increasingly chose to organize outside of formal city politics in order to develop a different form of politics including social mobilization and direct action. It is in this trajectory that we situate the following vignette. We begin with the Los Angeles Tenants Union (LATU).

The LATU was set up in 2015 on the back of a protest against gentrification. For most activists it became clear that the formal channels of political protest were not working.[45] Not necessarily because the political system is openly against vulnerable or poor people, but rather because its institutions and the people working within them cannot break the dominant property arrangements which are aligned against so many vulnerable and poor people. The strength of embedded interests around property in formal politics is such that politicians are extremely unlikely to break ranks and propose measures to upend the existing arrangements. Hence, it became obvious for housing activists that a different strategy was necessary to establish alternative practices of collective engagement and to counter processes of gentrification and displacement. The first step was to form a movement that would identify all housed and unhoused people as tenants and, from this, develop new forms of political coalition and action: 'In LATU we define a tenant as more than a renter. A tenant is anyone who doesn't control their housing.'[46]

This focus on the 'tenant' was crucial in order to delineate themselves from all those who own or control their own home. At the same time, it was an attempt to forge a political subjectivity and empower tenants to become agents of their own struggle. This is not a struggle focused on or occurring within the terrain of formal political institutions. It is rather about individuals developing a sense of themselves as political beings-in-common, forming collective interests and institutions across a range of spaces, from the single building to the neighbourhood. As one of the participants pertinently puts it:

> the focus is on learning what it feels like to become genuine, self-governing agents of change, transforming the world without relying on official political institutions or summoning the ultimately destructive forces of capital investment into our lives ... Each experience of self-government, each moment when tenants collectively take control over their everyday life, is an experience of the possibility of true participatory democracy.[47]

The LATU is embedded in a web of organizations with the shared aim of building 'insurgent grounds' in Los Angeles.[48] As in other cities, the focus is on the redistribution of wealth and property generated by enclosed urban spaces secured by private property regimes. For instance, the LATU calls for rent cancellation instead of just rent relief programmes, because only the former can significantly undermine power relations based on property regimes. Other parts of the wider movement occupy vacant houses or property owned by public entities, bringing these urban spaces back into use for those in need. The People's City Council LA was formed during the Covid-19 crisis as a response to the failure of the municipal government to protect the most vulnerable residents of LA from the impact of the pandemic. It is a project to connect and support all the various solidarity efforts on the ground. At the same time, it is also a testament to urban self-government and a collective acknowledgment that urbanites organize in different ways to cope with and de-couple themselves from the normalization of exclusion in urbanization encountered by many. By establishing parallel institutions of collective action, the People's City Council LA and the other organizations involved articulate a vision of urban collective life capable of addressing issues of public concern in meaningful ways. At the same time, these political actions also reveal that governmental institutions in Los Angeles are largely disconnected from the life worlds in which these collectives emerge.[49] For this reason, theirs is also a project of reconnecting politics to urban collective life.

Urban self-government

This chapter has depicted different claims for and practices of urban self-government in the realm of housing. On a very general level, the idea that all urbanites should participate in some way in the production of urban spaces is barely contested. But to relate this co-production of the urban to ideas and practices of self-government and ultimately democracy requires a step of the imagination. However, as we have shown through our examples, it is a step that activists around the world have already made. The notion of self-government, of directly participating in the governance of a space or resource, might often prompt qualifications or a 'but' such as: 'Of course, we should govern ourselves and the environment around us, but we need some formal structure that sets some limits or organizes the whole process.' Or: 'Yes, self-government is nice, but it's impossible to implement because not all those who are a part of that "self" can be assembled in one place or at one time.' It is true that there are pragmatic reasons to question the goal of self-government. But when we look around the globe we find numerous practices of urban self-government already in place. These are distinct from a strictly state form of politics, even in domains such as housing where the state traditionally plays a crucial part.

The episodes discussed above reveal a range of different modalities of urban self-government at work, as well as the different political strategies employed to achieve them. The position of the state is unquestionably crucial in this regard. Even a distinctly urban logic of self-government necessitates some engagement with the state as a (varying) source of political authority and progressive potential. In the Los Angeles case, this relation is a strictly antagonistic one, with the local state seen neither as a partner nor a source of democratic hope. In the cases of Berlin and Zurich, interaction with the state is less adversarial and the political vision driving the struggles incorporates a state transformed by urban society. In Zurich, the new housing cooperatives repositioned themselves as a political force distinct from but in close collaboration with the local state. This form of urban self-government is nested in more encompassing institutional structures. Housing cooperatives in Zurich are not as dependent on electoral political volatility as, for example, public housing is, but governmental changes in housing policy could still directly impact on their future workings. In Berlin, the struggle for urban self-government is played out largely on the terrain of the local state. But the ambition is not simply to build coalitions and change housing policy. Rather, since the concern is with how housing policy is made and by whom, it is a strategy aiming for democratization beyond the norms of formal politics. Remunicipalization is thus not an attempt to shift power from the market back to the state, but to elevate and embed urban society in new governance structures.

Reflecting on the self-governing strategies described above, we can be assured that alternatives to markets and states are very possible. These alternatives are generative of political subjects, instruments, relations and resources, albeit in different ways. Urban self-government centres on the claim to, aspiration for and practice of being involved in the processes of urbanization as such. There is a spatial immediacy discernible in urban self-government around housing, where citizens attempt to act directly upon spatial arrangements of the home. These practices therefore localize politics, making democracy a project of the everyday, graspable even if the forces arranged against it are far-reaching.

The act of actually self-governing – the effort to change how urbanization unfolds and to cope with the problems it induces – is situated in the here and now and not in distant administrative offices or the corridors of parliament. The forms of self-government discussed above articulate in different ways an immediate bodily relation to the built environment. Only when this happens, it seems, can the forces of urbanization be brought into reach for urban citizens and collectives. Only then are people able to intervene in and reappropriate the urban spaces they have been co-producing in the first place. But urban self-government is also a claim to govern differently. It is more about bringing material processes and people into resonance than establishing relations of sovereignty, even if the state remains a key player. Hence, we need to be mindful of affective practices through which the urban fabric becomes meaningful and a part of democratic projects.

One catalytic ground for urban self-government is property regimes. Politicizing, reformulating and relocating property bring together different, often separated, spheres of political action, such as the everyday and institutional formats of the state or markets, or of social organizations. At the intersections of these spheres, entanglements become visible and productive, and new forms of urban self-government can be developed. Urbanization is on most levels about transforming land, changing its uses and meanings; as a consequence urbanization also produces multifarious, unplannable externalities. But the magnitude of these externalities is hardly imaginable in advance or through scientific inquiry; they become real and articulated in and through everyday experience. This is why the spatial imaginary of the home is important in understanding the struggles around housing.

One – optimistic – reading of urbanization is that it is the history of turning apparently insignificant individual fates into problems of public concern. Claims for equality in urban collective life have much to overcome, from the hostility of contemporary neoliberal logics to the deeply embedded structures of power (based on property, wealth, etc.). But the political potential of urban space and its material resources remains. To really appreciate practices of self-government such as those mentioned here, we need to reconceptualize our own thinking of urban space, which is still largely a matter of rights based on ideas of sovereignty and state power. In many countries the legal framework of the state provides a distinct sphere where struggles over certain issues can be fought out in procedural settings intended to guarantee fairness and the absence of violence and sheer domination. This was and still is an achievement. Hence, the confrontation is not with the rule of law or legal rights per se, but rather with how these rights are distributed in the first place, and the scope of local autonomy they ensure. The point of urban self-government and of the wider urban project of democracy is not to deny this but to expand upon it – democratizing it further.

5

Urban Publics and Citizens

Who stands at the centre of democracy? The citizen. But how does somebody become a citizen? In democracies rooted in state frameworks, the answer to this question begins with the rights and institutions of those who belong to the political community of the nation: the people. But in an urban democracy the nation state is not the base, and rights and institutions are not the main anchors. In an urban democracy, citizenship is claimed and practised rather than legally granted. Returning to Wolin, democracy exists in the life force of the demos: the making of political subjects not in isolation but in conjunction with others. In this vision, the formation of the demos has something kinetic about it, as individuals not only come together but transform themselves, becoming more than the sum of their parts.[1] It is crucial to locate these moments when common causes are made and political subjects take shape. They are the basis of urban democracy, the times when the demos comes together. But how can citizenship be generated and organized in relation to a global process (urbanization) rather than a bounded community (the nation), and how can it be enacted in practices rather than laws and institutions?

The view presented here is that citizenship is made in the coming together of urban *publics*, the agents of a distinctly urban democracy. Urban publics are where democratic subjects are collectively conceived. These publics, we show, are not pre-existing or spatially pre-packaged; indeed, they are often not accounted for within existing political systems, not recognized as subjects of democracy by the state. Instead, our urban publics are engaged in diverse practices of being in and against urbanization, of seeking a place in urban collective life, of becoming urban citizens. The generation of publics occurs in mundane urban places and situations, as well as in the big moments of protests on the streets and in the squares. There are, of course, usually connections between such repertoires of politics. As Boudreau has argued, democratic projects require multiple forms of coming together and of making claims in order to counter the forces ranged against them.[2] Disparate as urban publics may be, a democratic imaginary of the city often underpins them, providing a locus around which networks of political activity can align across difference.

This chapter takes a journey through cities around the world, delving into emblematic cases. Publics are shown to be bubbling up within urban collective life, not fixed on a centre like the state, but dispersed through and roaming within urban processes. Beginning with the global cycling collectives of Critical Mass, we sketch out the parameters of urban publics.[3] Critical Mass collectives occupy roads, block normal flows of automobile traffic and prefigure an alternative hierarchy of urban transportation. Our goal is not to celebrate or romanticize Critical Mass as a particularly exceptional or effective form of political activism, but to use it to help expand our understanding of what urban democracy is or can be. Urban publics like Critical Mass reshuffle socio-spatial relations without making claims to sovereignty. This is a specifically urban way of being and becoming political, where practices, objects, bodies and ideas are brought together and related to urbanization.

From here, the second part of the chapter goes on to show that publics can constitute new forms of democratic citizenship embedded within urban collective life. Establishing alternative systems of urban everyday life can transform urban spatial practices, contesting exclusion, as well as advancing new forms of 'insurgent citizenship' based on belonging in the city.[4] Urban publics can be found in social centres, parallel institutions and a range of spatial practices not always understood as political. For those without state citizenship, like undocumented migrants, urban collective life becomes an alternative horizon of world-making and claiming. It also becomes a set of resources to be mobilized. Becoming an urban citizen, following Holston, rests on occupying the city, (re)making the city and making claims to belong in the city. Urban citizenship is advancing, alongside and in friction with national citizenship, particularly in the cities of the global south, though it is apparent also in cities of the global north. In this chapter, we consider how everyday claims to urban citizenship are related to other forms of democratic politics, such as urban movements and uprisings. Of course, our examples are dispersed and far from dominant, but they point to a different form of democracy aligning to urbanization. While not all-encompassing, they are nonetheless suggestive of ways in which urbanization can be democratized.

Puzzling Critical Mass

The scenes are familiar to many urbanites. From Manila to Montevideo, from Kiev to Los Angeles, cyclists gather every last Friday of the month to take the streets. Music, whistles, conversation between riders, varying degrees of confrontation with car drivers and pedestrians, varying degrees of ebullient behaviour, no leader, little sloganeering. But bodies in space, coming together, navigating the city. Critical Mass was established in San Francisco in the early 1990s and has spread across the globe as a distinct form of engaging with the streets and automobiles that structure the everyday experience of urban space.[5] There are of course differences between Critical Mass meetings in terms of their urban locations, the political significance of the routes cycled, the position of Critical Mass within wider networks of urban politics, and the scale, composition and ambition of the people participating. Yet, they all share some basic characteristics as a distinct urban way of acting collectively and politically. Critical Mass forces us to rethink how the gathering of urban citizens in space translates into publics, how these publics place themselves within the city as a political space and, further, how they challenge enshrined notions of citizenship and democracy.

Generally, Critical Mass has puzzled observers.[6] Are these gatherings and processions of cyclists constitutive of a social movement? If so, how can we understand its loose form of organization and its lack of clearly formulated claims? To whom is it even addressing its claims? Given that it does not engage directly with political institutions, can it even be seen as political? Put simply, what is the political effect of this practice? And what does it have to do with democracy? Certainly Critical Mass participants do not usually present themselves as political demonstrators, in a conventional sense, but there are political objectives in their 'celebration of the everyday'.[7] There is an obvious symbolism in riding through cities on bikes and disputing the subordinate position of cycling in relation to driving a car. But Critical Mass is also an experience of collective action, of bodies being together.[8] It performs an ecological and social alternative to the individualized car-dominated city, as well as establishing safer and self-organizing spaces for cyclists on the roads: safety through numbers instead of safety through separation. Crucially, the politics of Critical Mass is articulated in practices rather than words; it is a politics centred on access to and redistribution of space. It is not primarily about the representation of a view, interest or constituency, but about performing an alternative in the here and now.[9]

Being part of Critical Mass, or watching its participants passing by on the street, it seems clear that this moving assembly of colourful cyclists, bikes, sound machines, banners and voices constitutes some form of a public, and that it is also political in its intent. Critical Mass claims the streets as public space in order to make itself visible and audible. At the same time, it transforms the function and the meaning of the spaces it uses.[10] Yet, despite its visibility and volume, Critical Mass is often incomprehensible to existing political institutions. It remains hard to grasp because it defies key conventions of political behaviour, especially in relation to demonstrations and protest. Critical Mass does not speak with one voice; it has no proper place but is moving and merging. It does not address the formal political sphere with coherent claims or demands. Critical Mass points to the limitations of how we conceive democratic publics and, more generally, urban politics.

This becomes very obvious when courts and judges have to grapple with Critical Mass. Simon Parry tells the story of a legal case concerning Critical Mass London, though similar stories from cities all over the world could be recounted.[11] The London Metropolitan Police argued that Critical Mass had the obligation to notify them of the planned route of any rides because they amount to public processions and demonstrations. However, judges in a number of courts upheld – though not always unanimously – the view that Critical Mass rides must be considered common and customary practice, and were thus exempt from the notification conditions that political demonstrations and public processions must conform to. Parry recounts the considerations of one judge who argued that the most important formal aspect of Critical Mass was its spontaneous and disorganized constitution and route-finding. These characteristics, the judge argued, meant that it fell outside of the boundaries of the pertinent legislation: 'They involve gestures which were just not within the legislators' conception of public space.'[12] While Critical Mass, as a physical phenomenon, can be described in straightforward terms and can be reproduced across the globe, as a form of political activity it retains an elusive quality despite its expressiveness.[13]

The ambiguity of Critical Mass as a political and juridical object/subject is related to its position at the boundary of what is usually understood as political space. Critical Mass constitutes a public and a political subject which stands neither inside nor outside the established political space as defined mainly by the state and its institutions. As such, it fuels rather than resolves tensions between legality and extra-legality, between proper political agents and the seemingly ordinary, apolitical everyday life in towns and cities. It creates an interstitial space that escapes the standard definitions of protest and the binaries of ordinary/extraordinary so formative in thinking about politics. What is more, this space is created through the use and temporary occupation of actual urban space. As such, it locates and foregrounds a different understanding of political action and of democratic publics.

As Parry notes, however, 'Critical Mass makes itself visible, but what is made visible is clearly an illusion.'[14] Critical Mass is an illusion, though still real, because it acts as if city life can be altered in an immediate fashion without going through all the turmoil of the institutional politics of democratic decision-making. It is a performative critique of urban life.[15] And it is an illusion because it acts as if there were already a different symbolic political space in which these forms of publics have their proper democratic place and name. In both cases, then, Critical Mass provides an alternative idea of how to think about the relations between citizenship, publics and democracy.

Delineating urban publics

But what is an urban public in the first place and what kind of public is Critical Mass? On the most basic level, one might say, an urban public is a gathering of people, an assembly of citizens who are either addressed by political agents or who themselves address political agents. Kurt Iveson argues that the dominant – topographical – perspective on publics and public spaces delineates three different dimensions of publicness: a context of action (public space), a kind of action (public address) and a collective actor (the public/s).[16] In this view, all three dimensions are not only definable but also interlinked: the public as a somehow already existing actor addresses the formal political sphere through one voice in predefined public spaces. The relation between this idea of publics and formal politics is rational, discursive and confrontational. However, we concur with Iveson that the topographical approach to publics provides a limited view of what can happen in urban spaces around the globe. What is more, its vocabulary is of little help in grasping political acts like Critical Mass.

When we look at Critical Mass, the conventional idea of publics is problematized by the fact that the 'Mass' does not address others or speak with one voice. Indeed, it does not speak but rather makes a noise, and the noise it makes does not come from one voice. The context of action is, as the London judges concluded, blurred, and falls outside of the dominant legal understanding of public space (thus occurring in 'normal' urban space, presumably). Furthermore, the collective actor, the Critical Mass, is not really what is usually conceived of as *one* collective actor. Rather, Critical Mass is in line with Davina Cooper's understanding of a public that is not primarily formed through a circulation of address and attention between different actors.[17] Rather, it is first and foremost a peopled formation that comes-into-being as a public.[18] Publics emerge. And by becoming visible, by making issues and themselves public, they act upon existing conditions and create new spatial, social and political relations. From this perspective, publics cannot be envisaged only in terms of discourse and deliberation, but are conditioned by material infrastructures that they also act upon or even constitute. Publics are not spoken for, but have to '"come to voice", become embodied, generate the material and infrastructural conditions of their existence and find ways of expressing and enacting themselves'.[19]

This is also why publics are important in thinking about an urban democracy. As Judith Butler has argued, publics are always situated, the material environments in which they 'come to voice' are always part of the action, and 'they themselves act when they become the support for action'.[20] Political subjects, alliances or collectives cannot rely entirely on rights and pre-existing spaces. They always articulate and remake the spaces they use through their bodily practices. This of course opens up the possibility of emancipatory actions. Spaces can be re-inscribed by bodily practices. Spaces usually seen as private can be claimed as public. Spaces usually seen as apolitical (e.g. roads) can be claimed as political. Only through this kind of thinking can we make sense of the idea that democracy can happen everywhere and that democratic publics can emerge even in unlikely places. It is in this sense that Critical Mass is a performative gesture generating a space for urban citizenship and for the remaking of urban space.

The publics of urban collective life

Critical Mass is a visible and striking form of an urban public. It is also very fluid, transient. After all, the streets are taken just one Friday evening every month. In between, cars regain their dominance of the streets, and the rhythm of ordinary city life remains intact. This points to the limits of Critical Mass as an agent of political change. However, it is important to note that, in most places, Critical Mass is neither singular nor insular, but embedded in wider networks of politics and implicated in other urban publics. For instance, Critical Mass Madrid has had close links to other forms of urban politics. As in Rome, Los Angeles and many other places, the Madrid movement drew on the practices of activists in the city, linking especially to squatting culture and autonomous spaces. Bicycle workshops formed nodes in wider networks of not only active activists, so to speak, but also those whose political engagement was more limited, perhaps only to the monthly Critical Mass meetings.[21] This is suggestive of the ways in which alliances and common causes can be forged across differences. It points to the work involved in, the crafting of, urban publics. It lays bare the potential of urban collective life to be a plane of politics from which democratic claims can emerge and citizens can be made. If we squint our eyes a little, a vision of an urban form of democracy comes into view: publics forming through collective being/bodies in space, spatial practices and the use of the material resources at hand.

A brief consideration of squatting can help further delineate the democratic possibilities of such political practices. Like Critical Mass, squatting often does not involve putting claims to the state and waiting for a response. Squatters achieve their objectives in the immediacy of the act of squatting. Squatting links an everyday need (shelter, dwelling) and inequality (in housing), while breaking the law and wider socio-political relations. In an idealized form (and appreciating the variation in context and the contingencies of actions), it may be seen as short-circuiting the formal institutions of politics and law in order not only to realize an everyday need but also to assert alternatives to the institution of private property. Vasudevan has argued that squatting can potentially embody an alternative form of self-governing urbanity, what he terms the 'autonomous city'.[22] His study of squatting in Berlin details the changing everyday practices of the occupation of urban space that constitute squatting, showing their centrality to varying and wider urban struggles from the 1960s onwards, such as the struggle against gentrification. Critical Mass and squatting are both aimed at reshaping or reappropriating urban space. The means applied, the practices performed, are embedded within the everyday rhythms of city life. It is urban collective life directly engaging with existent urban spaces. Here it is important to note that these practices and collective acts should not be confused with private or individual desires and claims. Rather, both forms are purposely public in the sense that they are visible in public and make a claim to be recognized as a public alongside other urban publics.

In all cities there are networks of diverse urban publics. They are not always highly visible; indeed, seen through the state lens on politics they are not always considered properly political per se. But alongside more the obvious urban movements and protests, the following are apparent in most urban areas: social centres,[23] urban explorers,[24] dumpster divers,[25] community gardens,[26] alternative currencies and economic systems,[27] co-housing,[28] squatting,[29] 'empty spaces' movements,[30] 'space hijacking',[31] utility network hacking, and parallel institutions of, for instance, food provision and essential services like health and sanitation.[32]

Such practices can be deeply embedded in processes of establishing alternative urban systems of the everyday. Like a concrete utopia they try to realize a different world in the here and now, drawing on resources already present, but seeking to enact new social relations. Urban systems of the everyday are by their nature encompassing, entailing practices that are not rooted but circulate through urban space. A good example would be the various attempts to establish alternative urban food systems, linked to ideas such as food sovereignty, captured in practices such as food trading, dumpster diving, recovering disposed-of goods, and the more systematic notions of freeganism or foodsharing. These are attempts to avoid the norms of the food economy through improvisation and the generation of alternative forms of food organization. Similar interventions also include 'free-cycling', conducted through cooperatives and networks in which people can find and give goods as diverse as sofas or bikes.

To give just one example of urban food systems, Colleen Hammelman's rich research on seventy-two migrant women living in poverty – in Medellin, Colombia, and Washington DC, USA – shows how they have developed informal networks for growing and sharing food to deal with food insecurity.[33] Despite the differences between the two cities, the women were seen to employ similar everyday strategies to counter their exclusion from dominant urban systems and to deal with their poverty. These strategies are both individual and collective in the sense that they seek to advance an alternative provision of food. They included sharing and exchanging food in social networks, selling homemade goods, making use of food banks, reducing the variety of foods consumed, seeking governmental benefits, finding cheaper shops, buying in bulk and growing food.[34] Virtually all of the women drew on informal networks to acquire food, be they family, neighbours, friends, shop owners or employers. These networks are embedded in urban collective life, enacted through everyday practices, and draw in particular on nearby family and neighbours, those whom the women saw most often.[35] Additionally, they were not only focused on the needs of the women, the development of their common cause, but sometimes, particularly in Medellin, also developed into publics addressing problems within neighbourhoods (in relation to drug use) and offering more substantive alternative food systems (like urban gardens).[36]

Hammelman argues that common cause and organization emerged amongst the women in response to their lived experiences of 'exclusionary politics' and 'othering' rhetoric.[37] By countering their exclusion, the women were both making a claim to be part of the city and developing citizenship collectively amongst themselves. Their actions may have been a response to insecurity, and at first glance might be understood as forms of coping, self-help and even survival. But, as Hammelman shows, they are also political actions and democratic appeals.

In many places, such practices are indeed often driven by economic necessity, by the need to secure everyday provisions and basic services.[38] Not surprisingly, they spread as a reaction to austerity in Europe and North America, particularly in the wake of the global financial crisis of 2008/9, demonstrating how new alliances can be formed and maintained across different segments of the population.[39] Arampatzi details how, during a period of austerity in Athens, spatial practices to 're-appropriate certain areas of the neighborhood from exclusion and repressive tactics' gained increasing support from residents and community organizations.[40] These practices grounded in the everyday facilitated a 'politics of solidarity' which not only acknowledges differences but 'locates the strength of cooperation and solidarity among the multiple responses that can emerge to the same issue'.[41] Elsewhere, we have thought of such practices in terms of an 'urban everyday politics': collective, organized and strategic practices that articulate a political antagonism embedded in, but breaking with, urban everyday life by altering – however temporarily – time-and-place-specific social relations.

Such forms of politics can often become closely interlinked with other forms of politics. And yet, presenting urban collective life as the foundation of urban democracy raises questions. Might a politics of daily practices also risk being perceived as a form of exodus from real world politics into everyday utopias? Some of the practices described above, like Critical Mass, do not always provide democratic openings, even if they feed into Wolin's idea of cultivating and crafting democratic practices. Others, such as dumpster diving, might be just another distraction from confronting real problems head-on if they are not part of a more fundamental democratic claim to the city.[42] Against this background, the following section explores urban forms of 'insurgent citizenship' that counter the absence or denial of state citizenship, and in doing so foreground the city as a democratic alternative to the nation state.

The city and insurgent citizenship

City life is full of different forms of self-government and self-organization.[43] Some are more visible than others. Some articulate this complicated pattern of making things and issues public more directly and openly than others. What we have described so far are political practices mostly situated in and directed towards urban collective life. It is important to note that these practices are not on a different plane to 'real' politics. Rather, they engage in significant ways with institutional politics, which they may even transform in the process. The democratic idea of the city as an actual and virtual place plays a significant role in this.

Conventionally, democratic politics is about forming a collective will embedded in a predefined political community through a set of institutional rules. As understood here, democracy is more about the distribution of powers, capacities and possibilities for self-government across a heterogeneous and multi-layered urban society, where social or spatial boundaries are more blurred. These two logics of democratic politics can often exist alongside each other or even in ignorance of each other. Critical Mass is such an example. But in some cases, they collide or become entangled with each other. As we shall see, the two logics are often articulated in antagonistic terms, having their bases in different spatial-political contexts. On the one hand, there is city life, urbanity, as a context in which legal citizenship recedes from view and the stateless push their own claims to citizenship to the front of the political stage. 'Acts of citizenship' are key, and they are mostly embedded in ordinary spaces, prosaic encounters and everyday multiculturalism.[44] On the other hand, there are nation-state institutions and administrations which grant citizenship rights and provide arenas on different scales for the engagement of the people. This – to return to Wolin – is the predefined framework of equal rights gifted by an elite. These two logics are built on completely different understandings of politics and democracy. For the latter view, politics and democracy are bounded by a given set of rules and institutions which help to contain them. In the former view, democracy and politics are defined by their immanent capacity to forge new ways of organizing and alternative modes of self-rule, where the self is never bounded and fixed.

For Isin, this is why the city is so important for democracy. He calls the city a difference machine because it both produces new differences and is also a space where those differences can be negotiated.[45] It stands in confrontation with the nation state which posits and demarcates from above, without much room for manoeuvre, who belongs, who has political rights, who obtains the status of citizenship. It is in this field of tension that we situate our example of urban citizenship, through which we discuss how making things public not only reframes our understanding of citizenship but may also provide a strategy to transform relations to and within the state. Urban citizenship so understood is a different vision of how individuals are related to the collective. You are a citizen because you are here in the actual space of the city, you belong to the city and are a city-maker, and because of this you claim rights to the city. Citizenship becomes an act of belonging to urban collective life and thus to the city. Publics are the collectives through which individuals become urban citizens, asserting their right to belong to the city even if they cannot formally belong to it. Here we see the city as both an actual and a virtual place. The city provides the very grounds of democratic politics and is the democratic imaginary evoked in rights-claiming. It is the bonding element on the symbolic level, denoting a different way of doing politics and democracy, a different way of becoming a citizen.

A similar line of argument has been developed by Holston. He argues that the resurgence of the 'city' as a locus of political citizenship, particularly in the global south, is being driven by the confluence of forces running through global urbanization. His work on 'insurgent citizenship' hones in on how urbanites are reimagining what it means to be a democratic citizen in contemporary cities. In recent decades the varied interlinkages between urbanization, democratization and neoliberalism have generated new conditions of political opportunity and constraint for many. As cities of the south grow, citizenship is denied not only to migrants but also to those with formal citizenship who are nevertheless excluded from the spaces of prosperity and comfort within the city. In response, a growing number of urbanites have engaged in practices of insurgent citizenship. This urban form of citizenship emerges at the intersections of city-making, city-occupying and rights-claiming.[46] The inequalities, injustices and exclusions generated by surging capitalist urbanization are not the backdrop but the very grounds of urban citizenship. The urban poor of the global south are making claims to the city, but a city differently distributed.[47]

Claims to urban citizenship are in many ways made outside the normative, legal and institutional frameworks of the state. In the absence of possession, urban citizenship rests on acts, claims to belonging, and gaining access to the amenities required for a decent life, like housing, sanitation, health services, education and child care. Rights are claimed in concert with others – in publics – and held in common with others.[48] Political rights are no longer possessed or distributed by the state, and no longer conceived individually, but are achieved through the coming-togethers of urban publics, through the shift from being an individual to being a part of a collective. Urban publics (and not the state) are the generators of insurgent citizenship. And urbanization is foregrounding the 'city' as an alternative to the political locus of the state. Hence, insurgent citizenship is not about belonging to the community of the nation; rather, it is about being in urban publics and belonging to the city.

But how do citizens take form, how are urban publics mobilized, how is the 'city' evoked as a collective project? We would say: through practices. Recent urban scholarship has captured the diversity and extent of democratic claims to citizenship in the city. Whether they take the form of protest movements, occupations, negotiations or more discrete non-movement type actions, the common thread linking them is that they are situated in everyday experiences of urban life, often driven by a 'collective sense of aspiration or disenfranchisement'.[49]

In his work on Brazilian cities, Holston shows that over recent decades urbanites have been struggling for new forms of citizenship, which he characterizes as being primarily about the struggle for the 'city' itself, rather than, say, the struggle of labour.[50] Holston's work de-centres the classical 'city', imagined as the inner city, and points instead to the 'peripheries' of informality, heterogeneity and ambiguous legal statuses. Thus, while the 'city' may be at the centre of these publics as a stake, it is not the classically dense inner centre. It is the de-centred city understood in terms of the moments, spaces and places of urbanization, and as the imaginary of democracy.

Colin Macfarlane and Jonathan Silver make a similar claim about the development of the 'urban political' in their 'Poolitical City' article.[51] Here urban publics and political rights-claiming are entwined with the materialities of the everyday worlds of the city, in this case, the infrastructures of waste in Cape Town, South Africa. Macfarlane and Silver show how the politicization of human waste not only makes public the racial and social inequalities of sanitation infrastructures, but is constitutive of an urban politics. As they put it, it is 'vital to the production of the urban political itself'.[52] They identify the tactics and spatial-political practices through which publics are mobilized, including 'spectacle', 'auditing' and 'sabotage'.[53] Spectacle was achieved by Cape Town's 'poo protests', during which shit was thrown by residents of informal settlements at strategically selected sites such as the city airport.[54] This 'politicization of the city', in which the anger at its inequalities was laid bare, was accompanied by the much less dramatic auditing of toilet conditions in the area of Khayelitsha.

Adopting the language of the state to hold it to account, the auditing entailed the generation of a *poolitical* public – including the auditors, those involved in 'maintenance, operation, and repair',[55] those receiving information about the toilets they frequented, and related connections and common causes drawn between people across the area. Sabotage of infrastructure, common in the anti-apartheid struggle, was also employed, with the breaking of toilets a material and visible articulation of grievance, provoking the state into name-calling: its claims of 'vandalism' were countered with demands for better state funding for sanitation.[56] Spatial practices of this sort, intentionally illegal, also generate publics and delineate opponents, making political claims as they intervene in urban space and demarcate a terrain of struggle. Also in relation to infrastructure politics in Cape Town, Charlotte Lemanski argues that 'illegal' or 'uncivil' acts (such as throwing shit) are viewed by many urbanites as legitimate forms of 'citizenship-in-action' in a 'context of rapid urbanisation and poverty'.[57]

More recently, Holston has argued that insurgent claims to citizenship have come to characterize politics in the cities of the global north as well as the south, following the urban uprisings and movements of the 2010s, and the growing sense of exclusion and injustice within cities in the wake of the global financial crisis.[58] These protests were grounded in the changing (very often deteriorating) conditions of urban collective life in places like the UK, the USA, Greece and Spain. In other words, it is no longer only those without formal citizenship claiming urban citizenship. The protests, riots and movements point to very visible forms of urban publics, along with the less spectacular kinds mentioned in the preceding section. The city, Holston claims, 'offers an emerging alternative for a different kind of political community', a place where social life can be thought in common, where the city as a commons can act as a world commons.[59]

Holston argues that, ultimately, global urbanization, from the south to the north, has 'transformed Lefebvre's conceptual frame of right to the city by articulating it as a right of urban citizenship, in which the primary ground of this citizen right is belonging to the city and not the nation state'.[60] The urban uprisings and movements of the 2010s were, of course, diverse, but they shared the characteristic of being a struggle for the city: 'They struck at the city itself, not the factory or government building as in previous centuries.'[61] The urgency, register and scale of the uprisings was very different to those of most Critical Mass meetings, but the use of bodies in urban space – to utilize and occupy its spaces of circulation, meeting and meaning – is indicative of an urban, spatialized form of democracy. In many cases, the protestors were making demands of the state to intervene, to improve and extend rights, but many other protests made no appeal to the state at all.[62] Here, issues of housing and mobility were no longer simply policy issues or local problems; they were the defining issues of politics and the issues through which democratic claims were conceived.

The urban resources of democracy

Urban forms of democracy, we contend, are rooted in engagements with urban collective life, whatever repertoires of political action may emerge. Konstantinos Roussos's reflections on the politics of austerity in crisis-ridden Greece in the 2010s emphasize how political subjectivities emerged through a 'repoliticization of everyday life', where diverse publics emerged in collective action inspired by the vision of the commons.[63] The social medical centres, homeless support networks, social groceries, time banks and so on – which constitute alternative, non-state systems of collective life – are closely related to the 'squares movement' of 2011, during which diverse occupations and popular assemblies in cities emerged to contest the austerity measures forced on Greek society by their own national government (as well as the European Commission, the European Central Bank and the International Monetary Fund).[64]

This was a moment in which democratic politics really was enacted by urbanites – in Athens, in other Greek cities and in cities across southern Europe and beyond. Streets and squares were occupied, used as stages, stakes and sources of democracy. In Athens' Syntagma Square, two different movements were apparent, one more nationalistic, the other more inclusive, and in dialogue.[65] The latter was not simply about protest, or putting demands to the nation state and beyond. It could be seen as the democratic idea of the city coming to life. It was a democratic exchange, involving the formation of publics, standpoints, and their contestation, and the linking of local networks and needs with wider claims as the movements of the moment entwined with pre-existing activist and neighbourhood networks. As mentioned in Chapter 4, the political platform Barcelona en Comú emerged in the wake of the squares movement, drawing together an array of urban publics, from long-established housing groups campaigning against rising evictions in the city, to the activists of the square looking to sustain the movement in more institutionalized forms. We will discuss this and other cases of movement-state interaction in Chapter 6, where its limits as well as its possibilities are made clear. But the point to emphasize here is that these different repertoires of political action revolve around urban collective life, as a locus of democratic ideas and practices.

Urban collective life can generate new places of democratic action in direct response to urbanization and can constitute networked publics which are actual and bodily. As such, it can shape political subjects and their understandings of citizenship, as well as challenge ideas about how publics are formed and how they address state spaces. It is a very material form of politics, generating publics and places of democratic action through spatial practices. This form of politics is more closely related to other forms, like social movements, than is frequently recognized. Indeed, urbanity, urban collective life, is much closer to protest politics than is often thought. Julie-Anne Boudreau, Nathalie Boucher and Marilena Liguori call attention to this interrelatedness in their article on immigration movements in Los Angeles, 'Taking the Bus Daily and Demonstrating on Sunday', which emphasizes the grounding of large movements and mobilizations in the everyday interactions between urbanites.[66] This might include taking the bus, developing a shared sense of exclusion with other travellers in a similar position, and then moving on from this to a shared sense of purpose in addressing that exclusion through collective action. It might also involve the very fabric – material and virtual – of city life.

Thinking about democracy in this way forces us to consider urban collective life as a crucial condition for democratic mobilization. Based on a comparative historical examination (1970–2015) of how immigrant rights movements have been entwined with urban spatial practices and struggles in the cities of Amsterdam, Paris and Los

Angeles, Walter Nicholls and Justus Uitermark show that the potential for publics lies deep within the urban conditions of proximity, density and mass (number of people).[67] From everyday encounters in neighbourhoods to political meetings to the strategic development of wider networks, urban settings provide 'relational resources' which can turn small groupings into large mobilizations, transforming individuals into citizens.[68]

If urban collective life can provide an array of resources for democratic politics, there are also limits and contingencies. The resources are not simply there, lying in store, waiting to be picked up and used. As Nicholls and Uitermark argue, they have to be generated, which requires work, organization, strategic thinking, alliance building, and resources of time and knowledge. Furthermore, urban conditions vary and change, and can become more or less conducive to enacting publics. And the urban itself is contested. For instance, Nicholls and Uitermark describe the city as a field of contention between instruments of government and those complying with, resisting or ignoring them.[69] Obviously governments are aware of the political potential of certain urban places. They do their utmost to know, remake and control them. They try to disrupt and neutralize the potential of these places by making them objects of government policy. Since the reach of the state in urban space is impossible to fully escape, it must be engaged with politically. The same is true of the market, as the following example shows.

Leandro Minuchin and colleagues' study of the impacts of the Covid-19 pandemic on the residents of Rosario, Argentina, highlighted the extent to which urban life is not only dependent on diverse infrastructures and its rhythms of consumption, work, leisure and so on, but is entirely unimaginable without them.[70] The disruption caused by the pandemic exposed further the privatized and commodified forms of ownership and supply in the economy and the inequalities that are entwined with them. Minuchin et al. show how, with procurement and supply chains (of food and medical supplies for example) severely disrupted by the pandemic, infrastructural logistics became a matter of public debate: 'how are things moved? Who controls the platforms that organize virtual spaces of exchange? Are there ways of intervening in supply chains?'[71]

Opposition grew to the commodification of platforms and distribution channels, and the urban, rather than the national, became the arena in which the problems were situated and political action located. This was not because health or food policies were formally a matter of local or city governments, but rather because it became clear that new infrastructural arrangements could only be tried and tested in situations of urban collective life, where services had to be integrated and food and medicines were needed.[72] Political alternatives and coping measures also emerged from urban collective life, with local solidarity networks growing to deal with the gaps in goods and services. What was laid bare during this period was the absolute entwining of scales, global and local, and of places near and far, through the infrastructures of global urbanization.[73] Minuchin et al. make the crucial point that this is not only the context of city life but also provides the political conditions in which politics and democracy can be situated.

> The civic imaginations that associated city life with fleeting encounters, where political parties and democratic confrontations organized the margins and reach of social and economic rights, are replaced by territorialities where urban identities are forged around residents' ability to become enmeshed with distribution chains, exchange platforms or solidarity networks.[74]

This is the global urban politics Boudreau has identified, one shaped by the practices, processes and places of global urbanization, as much as by voting, joining political parties or large-scale urban mobilizations.[75] In our terms, these are the conditions in which the idea of the democratic city needs to be resituated, at a distance to the state, in the midst of urban collective life. The point to emphasize here is that the socio-materiality of urban collective life is not incidental to the forms of politics which emerge from it, and is not even only an object of contestation – it can shape the entire logic of political and democratic action.

The proliferation of such publics and the linkages that often occur between them are indicative of the networked, non-sovereign and de-centred form of urban politics we detailed in Chapter 2. These publics may be diverse, but they can be seen to be making common cause through urban self-government rather than the state. Urbanity and not the state, as Boudreau argues, can provide the conditions of political action.[76]

Democracy and urban collective life

The preceding chapter focused primarily on practices of urban self-government, the 'what' of urban democracy and how it can be enacted. This chapter has been more concerned with the 'who' of urban democracy, its publics and citizens. Urban publics challenge scalar logics of state-based political organization and the legal understandings of citizenship underpinning it. City life is a material and social source, site and stake. It becomes the frame of reference or horizon within which political agents take shape, make common cause and seek collective action and organization. The urban publics which prompt these claims can be seen as alternatives to, and contestations of, the institutions of the state. But how can they sustain themselves, and an urban democracy, if they appear to rely on everyday practices rather than established institutions, on unpredictable resonances across social differences and urban space, on the difficult work of aligning bodies in space at particular times?

The urban publics of the streets and squares, of Critical Mass, or of the waste systems of Cape Town are, like the demos itself, flourishes of collective action, sense and organization. They have an insurgent or fugitive quality, as Wolin would say, but that does not mean that the democratic politics of the city exists only in these moments. Rather, there are social and material resources on which such urban publics can form. They have to be mobilized of course, but it is possible to see social centres, squats, neighbourhood housing groups and so on, as part of what Wolin would have called a broader democratic consciousness enacted through practices, citizenship claiming and making places of democracy. They are often transient, loose and unpredictable – but not always. Urban resources can be collectively organized and the political potential to act built into neighbourhood networks, social movements and even the regular everyday interactions through which shared causes are forged.

Even in the moments of uprising where the kinetic energy of urbanity is most politically vital, these residual and stored resources are important to the generation of publics and citizenship claims. Organization and strategic action are paramount when it comes to tapping into such resources as well as fostering the dynamism of the demos coming together. This is made clear in Omar Robert Hamilton's novelized account of the uprising in Cairo in 2011, *The City Always Wins*.[77] He draws on his involvement in events to paint a picture of how activists stoked the spontaneity; as people emerged into the streets and the square of Tahir, they drew on existing organizations and saw the opportunities of the city as a political stake, source and site. The key point to make is that urban collective life provides the condition of possibility for urban publics, the resources upon which democratic movements nourish themselves. This is not a democratic politics confined to dissensus and occasional crystallization in 'events', as stylized in so much recent political thought. Rather, the legwork of democratic politics involves a 'commoning of solidarities', where the resources of urban collective life feed into the making of alliances, marked by trust and caring, talking as well as disagreement, contention and moments of upheaval.[78]

Urban political life is always bubbling away, an enmeshed set of assemblages, chafing and wriggling for space and voice. Everyday encounters are crucial – talking, connecting and making plans can develop a common cause and forge collective action. Developing urban publics and citizens is a thoroughly socio-material process that depends on 'the ability of residents to engage complex combinations of objects, spaces, persons, and practices'.[79] We have noted that these offer an alternative political terrain on which urban publics and citizens are made. The state is decentred here, still a player, but not the sun around which everything revolves. Instead, the horizon of urban democracy is characterized by publics making common cause and forging collective decision-making organizations with the 'city' as the horizon of citizenship and democracy.

This brings us, inevitably, back to the state and the paradox outlined in Chapter 3: that democracy can never be achieved through, or embodied within, the state, but the state can never be escaped. How then can democracy flourish, advance and persist? The state must be engaged in some form, but how? What does adopting an 'interstitial distance' to the state mean in terms of locating democratic projects? This chapter has shown how publics draw on the socio-materiality of the 'urban' as the places of democracy. Urban collective life offers opportunities to recede from the state view, but urban publics and citizens can never vanish altogether. The following chapter explores how urban democracy can be located at interstitial distances to the state.

6

Urban Democracy and the State

Democracy always requires a location, a place where collective self-government can be situated, enacted in practices and publics. In the previous chapter we argued that urban democracy is located within urban collective life and can be roaming and unruly as people seek common cause and organization. But the state haunts the possibility of such a democracy. The state can pull politics towards itself, squashing out to the margins any politics it sees as a threat. It can rationalize and order in the name of peace. It can legislate, shape debates and use violence to transform how urban spaces are made and governed. The potential reach of the state – its power, both visible (police, administrative buildings, etc.) and invisible (laws, imaginaries of sovereignty) – permeates everyday life. Of course, the potency of the state varies across the globe, but its mythology often obscures the contingency of its power and the ways in which global urban politics is driving the informalization of the state.[1] Nonetheless, there is no doubt that the state cannot simply be ignored. So, how can urban democracy flourish in this context? How should democracy engage with the state?

In this chapter we argue that strategic engagements with the state are not only unavoidable, but potentially useful to projects of democracy, and that there are contemporary examples from which we can draw inspiration. We return to the democracy/state paradox (as outlined in Chapter 3), which must be confronted but can never be resolved. This may therefore initially seem a fruitless way of considering strategies of democracy. However, it is the very irresolvability of the paradox that is essential to the delineation of democratic projects. The paradox is that the state can never be the harbinger or host of democracy, but it can in no way be fully escaped or avoided. Democratic politics will always be contingent on engagements with the state. Places of democracy will, inevitably, witness the entanglement of both contradictory conditions – the urge to get beyond the state and the inability to finally escape its reach. There is no single or ideal way of dealing strategically with the state; there is only the contingent, situated politics of democracy. But the guiding force for engagements with the state is clear – the creation of non-sovereign political contexts, or places, in which collective self-government can prosper. Within such contexts the state is de-centred, reduced to an enabler or partner at the side of the demos.

We return first to Critchley's idea that democracy entails an interstitial or internal distance to the state. On a conceptual level this means there is no definitive binary between state and society; that urban democracy, or collective self-rule, is not restricted to a realm called 'society', because there can be no pure, distinct realm or entity like the state. There is instead a 'democracy/state nexus':[2] a series of potential entanglements between democracy and the state, a terrain of contradictions and mutual production. Necessarily, given the meeting of the contrasting logics of the state and the self-governing demos, the nexus rests on the irresolvability of the paradox. If, following Cooper, the notion of the nexus breaches the conceptual and normative boundaries between state and society, on an empirical and strategic level it also denotes that there is no simple or single strategy to deal with the state, no simple or single distance to the state, and no simple or single location for a democratic project in relation to the state. The state should be seen as a terrain of social struggle, with contingent and morphing reaches of power.[3] A project of democracy will always entail an answer to the question: to what purpose(s) can the state be put?[4]

To guide us in the task we look to emergent projects of the new municipalist movement, centred most prominently on Barcelona. More generally, after the urban uprisings of the early 2010s in which the streets and squares took political centre stage, there has been a marked (re)turn to occupying the institutions of the state.[5] The state is back, or so it seems, as a possibility for democratic movements. The new municipalism is many things, but one of its main features is a productive if strategic engagement with the state in an attempt to overcome what Gianpaulo Baiocchi vividly describes as the lack of communication between 'two separate worlds': the 'vibrant world of movements and mobilization, and the sterile and uninspired world of political parties'.[6] Baiocchi was writing about Latin America in the 1990s and 2000s, when cities led the way in forging claims for urban democracy. These projects were very different from the traditional municipalism centred on the local state, highlighted in Chapter 1. Indeed, we might now see them as precursors to the new municipalism of a decade or so later.[7] Across the region, from Montevideo to Mexico City, from Santos, Brazil, to Ilo, Peru,[8] state governments were taken over by figures with close ties to social movements, who opened state institutions to citizen participation and implemented progressive policies. Porto Alegre was perhaps the most emblematic case.[9] What was striking about these 'Radical Cities' was that they collapsed the boundaries between political parties and social movements, and, in the process, sought to transform the state into a facilitator of self-governance and a terrain for democratization.

The ultimate potential of the new municipalist projects of today lies in their positive embrace of the democracy/state nexus and its staging on the democratic horizon of the city.[10] If, as we have argued, the city is where the political opportunities of urbanization are grasped, it is also where the democracy/state nexus plays out and is generative of contingent democratic politics. To illuminate this potential, the chapter first returns to the idea of the democracy/state nexus in order to collapse the binary between state and society. On this basis, we detail four municipalist projects that each locate themselves in differing ways to the state: Preston (UK), Co-operation Jackson (USA), Barcelona (Spain) and Naples (Italy). The stances they adopt towards the state are productive of democratic possibilities and limits. Accepting that all projects of democracy will be contingent, our purpose is less to critique the new municipalism on its own terms, and more to engage positively with the conundrums it raises in relation to democratic strategies towards the state.

The democracy/state nexus

One of the main overarching arguments of this book is that a conceptual and normative disentangling of, first, politics and, then, democracy from the state is required if we are to realize the project of the city. However, it is now necessary to consider why this disentangling will always be contingent and incomplete. In Chapter 3 we outlined Critchley's idea that democracy must find an interstitial distance to the state. This, we argued, dealt with the dilemma we confront when considering how to position democracy in relation to the state. Historically, the state has often been the enemy of democracy, the instrument of dominant societal forces.[11] The state's variable and contingent power to make policy and to produce knowledge about the world can never alone be the resource on which democracy is made and persists, as Wolin so strongly argued. Yet, at the same time, in many places the state has established the conditions for broader political participation and for the equal treatment of people (however limited its definition of the 'people'). The state cannot be perceived as being simply the instrument of capital. As we discussed in Chapter 1, the (municipal) state was an enabler of democratic projects, even if ultimately its limits as a field of political action were exposed. On the face of it, the logic at play seems to bring us to an either-or situation: either democracy exists outside of the state or there is no democracy; either the state is enrolled in democratic projects or they are destined to fail.

Critchley's move, whereby any distance from the state remains within or internal to the state, helps us deal with this through its embrace of the need for apartness and acceptance of its ultimate impossibility. Critchley, however, does not really go further in providing ideas as to what the state might be able to positively offer. To address this deficit, we can ourselves take his argument a step further and posit that if democracy can only exist at interstitial distances to the state, then there can be no democracy outside of the state. There is, then, no location external to the state, be it spatial-material or imaginative-theoretical, where democracy can be placed. Of course, this sounds like it contradicts the aim of disentangling democracy from the state. But the purpose here is to accept, and hold in suspension, the tension between the two. It is about embracing the democracy/state nexus, as Kohn encourages us to do.[12] This entails, further, an openness to the forms that engagements with the state can take: they might be opportunistic as well as oppositional; and an oppositional stance towards the state might necessarily – and positively – incorporate elements of the state. Acting in direct opposition to the state may, paradoxically, entail becoming defined by its parameters, reifying them even. To deal with this, we propose that the state itself should be approached in an opportunistic way, guided by a sense of its fluidity as well as fixity, a sense that it can change when democratic projects engage with it.

Embracing the tension in the democracy/state nexus is thus the only way to deal with the paradoxes and conundrums it generates. If democratic projects are diverse in form, the state too should not be seen as a monolithic bloc, but rather as internally varied and heterogeneous, structured by forces that push it in different directions.[13] Such a stance recognizes the state's presence but does not enter a fixed friend or enemy position. Rather, it accepts that the state may be useful and that it can, in places and in parts, be incorporated into democratic projects.[14] A different horizon of political action opens up, where the key question is not what the state is but rather to what democratic purposes it can be put. The notion of always being, simultaneously, dialectically, 'in, against and beyond the state' is useful here.[15] It suggests not only diverse engagements with the state but also that the state can have diverse characteristics, that elements of it can be enrolled in democratic projects, however much tension there is due to the state's political importance, powers and pathologies. The idea of interstitial distances to the state problematizes the notion that democratic movements have to decide whether to locate themselves inside, alongside or in opposition to the state.[16] The view presented here is that engagements may incorporate all three positions. What is crucial is that they always seek an interstitial distance and that they do not submit to the state logic of democracy, whatever compromises may unfold.

In fleshing out what such a nexus implies for democratic politics, the work of Cooper is very useful. She has also engaged the idea of the nexus to get beyond what she identifies as the false binary between democratic political publics, on the one hand, and the state and its institutions on the other.[17] Three elements of her work are important for our purposes here. First, the nexus denotes the networks which emerge around political projects at the fringes of and even within state formations. Second, these projects may entail taking up or drawing upon state-generated resources. Third, the nexus idea emphasizes the extent to which the state shapes life and hence the extent to which logics of the state and alternative logics merge as well as diverge. For us, this captures nicely the indivisibility of the state and society, even when democratic projects align against the state or seek autonomy from it.

Cooper's work is fascinating in taking seriously the connections between the state and society, seeing them as generative grounds for a transformative democratic politics. She focuses directly on the meeting points, 'their fusion, attachment, and incorporation rather than their separation'.[18] Indeed, her definition of the state emphasizes its fluidity and permeability; the state may be one of many terrains of political struggle but it is not a unitary actor or a one-dimensional thing. Instead, the state is riven by social forces seeking power and legitimacy – as well as meaning – within it. Ultimately, the state can be, and has been, a part of democratic projects; in the UK for example: 'For lesbians, gay men, feminists, and other progressive forces, the state has proved in recent years a key site of engagement.'[19]

Cooper's work can be understood as opening up a thoroughly strategic approach to the state. Indeed, she emphasizes that while the state may not be the answer to the problem of democracy, the lack of a clear division between state and non-state practices and politics means that the state's powers to plan, redistribute and make binding decisions should never be abandoned to elite and dominant interests. The inevitable result of such an abandonment is that the state will be lined up against projects of democratic transformation. But Cooper's point is not simply about the need to occupy the institutions of the state. By not reifying the state, she opens up the possibility that it can be repurposed, not only in terms of its institutional structure, but also in terms of what it 'means to be a state: specifically, what states do, what makes them up, and how they interface with other aspects of the social'.[20] She argues there are many possible states; that there is no single essentialized version of the state because it is, to some extent, the outcome of the forces competing for it. From this perspective, the state does not have to be conceived as only sovereign and bureaucratic, nor only as the tool of the socially dominant. Even if it often is this, it is not this alone – it exists in its multiple purposes, politics and practices. Taking inspiration from the geographer Gibson-Graham's work on the economy, Cooper argues that it is possible to reimagine the state as it already is, not as some idealized new form in a 'forward looking' (rather than backward facing) prefigurative conceptualization of the state.[21] The implications for democratic projects are clear: they are not only grounded in, but are shaped by and terminate in, contingent political conditions. Democracy does not have a clean slate to work with or an unadulterated future ahead of it. Democratic projects operate on multi-layered grounds and within plural relations to the state. There are indeed various relations possible between state and society given the extent to which the state is linked to everyday life. Cooper reminds us that we need to be more imaginative regarding the purposes to which the state can be put in rendering its political potential.[22] To the idea of the nation state she adds 'guerrilla, micro, city, regional and global states'.[23] Being imaginative, we might add to this list the 'urban state', one that engages in a non-sovereign politics and advances collective self-rule.

Four interstitial distances to the state

In this section, we draw on four distinct projects of new municipalism to delineate a range of distances to the state and highlight the possibilities and limits they entail. Throughout, our arguments turn on the paradox born of the meeting of two contradictory impulses: on the one hand, the democratic necessity of grounding democracy apart from the state, without it ever becoming a project of the state; and, on the other hand, the strategic compulsion to engage with the state as an unavoidable and potentially productive range of forces. Throughout, we ponder the extent to which urban democracy can prefigure a new form of the state.

The Preston Model: stuck in city hall

Preston, a post-industrial city of around 115,000 inhabitants in north-west England, has been much-lauded in recent years as an example of a resurgent local state. It has even earned its own label, the 'Preston Model'. A stronghold of the Labour Party, the city council's leadership has become most closely associated with policies like community wealth building, a local economic development strategy aiming for more 'collaborative, inclusive, sustainable, and democratically controlled local economies'.[24] Since 2013, the council has been enrolling key local organizations (such as the University of Central Lancashire) as 'anchor institutions', with a set of agreements aimed at keeping wealth within the city region and advancing fairer practices of employment and better working conditions. Focused on directing the procurement practices of large local organizations to local suppliers, this approach was developed in close cooperation with progressive policy think-tanks like Democracy Collaborative, based in the United States, and the Centre for Local Economic Strategies, based in the UK. Alongside the flagship policy of community wealth building, the Preston Model also places emphasis on supporting cooperatives as a way of democratizing the economy and service provision. The council is committed to finding ways to support and establish 'worker co-operatives, community land trusts, community development finance institutions, so-called "anchor" procurement strategies, municipal and local public enterprise, participatory planning and budgeting'.[25]

The basic impulse of this project is to push back against extractive and corporate-controlled global urbanization, as well as the norms of neoliberal policy, such as public-private partnerships and private finance initiatives, which characterize so many urban areas. The aim is to supplant these market-based economic institutions with diverse institutional forms of collective ownership and participation. By 2017 the Preston Model had increased anchor institution spending in the city's economy from £38 million to £111 million.[26] Given the challenges facing this post-industrial region, such as significant numbers of low-income households and unemployment, much of the admiration for what is happening in Preston stems from the city council's clear ambition in a context that allows little room for policy manoeuvre. Severe austerity in England, initiated by the national government in the wake of the global financial crisis of 2008/9, has led to local government budgets being cut by around 50 per cent since 2010.[27] Many councils have had to make drastic cuts to their services, which have impacted most heavily upon poorer and marginalized sections of society.[28] Given this, the Preston Model might be welcomed as an attempt to ensure that basic services and life conditions are supported by the local state as an intervening and facilitating force.

For all its many merits, however, the Preston Model is limited as a project of democracy, as understood here. It remains city-hall-centred and statist, seemingly closer to the old municipalism than any form of new municipalism. Matthew Thompson has made similar observations in a piece about Preston and other ongoing municipalist projects in the UK, like Salford.[29] The Preston Model does not entail an attempt to shift the logic of doing politics and democracy in the here and now. Rather, it is a project of engaging with the state, wielding the power of policy to generate the conditions for more democratic futures. While the council leader, Matthew Brown, recognizes the need for increased citizen participation in Preston, and is correct to point out that the city does not have the vibrant urban activism found in some other places, he nevertheless still comes across as a little defensive in tone and circumspect about the merits of building movements with citizens.[30]

In terms of the democracy/state nexus and the idea of interstitial space, the Preston Model appears quite comfortable within state institutions, and too conservative in its ambitions to advance democracy. If we accept that democracy can never really be external to the state, the Preston Model need not be criticized for having its origins in a political party (the Labour Party) and the office of the local state (Preston City Council), because democratic projects will always be contingent and will play out in unpredictable, very context-specific ways. Furthermore, a democratic project can, in theory, emerge within the state, and can certainly encapsulate aspects of it. The critique that can be made of Preston is that it does not really seek to generate the demos, to take politics out of state institutions and into the places of urban collective life. This hesitancy to work across the state-society binary is a familiar weak point of municipalist projects, certainly in the UK. The city councils of the 1980s led by the 'new urban left' in places like London and Sheffield also struggled to decentralise political power whilst also working with(in) the state, to transform it by way of a new form of democratic 'local socialism'.[31] As we shall see below, however, there are contemporary cases that point to the continuing potential of operating within the democracy/state nexus.

Thompson has called projects like Preston 'managed municipalism', in which the municipal urban scale is harnessed to promote other forms of more democratic political organization.[32] We might see these diverse organizational forms as providing inspiration for a future urban state, a striking mosaic of cooperatives and collectives, from local banks to food suppliers and cafes, enmeshed with the state in the development of a localized urbanization. But, at present, this is a work-in-progress. Alternative visions of the relationship between democracy and the state do not have to be deferred, but can be practised and prefigured.

Preston remains an institutionalist vision of democracy, and a rather fixed one, which can be contrasted to the examples of Barcelona and Naples. In Preston, the state is still irremovably central, sovereignty is sought and democracy is thoroughly representative.

Cooperation Jackson: democracy in parallel to the state

In contrast to Preston, Cooperation Jackson is a movement: a citizen-led project of socialism, shaped by ideas of Black self-rule, aiming to organize and empower 'the structurally under and unemployed sectors of the working class, particularly from Black and Latino communities'.[33] It seeks a clear distance to, a space apart from, the state in the collective organizational forms it develops. Cooperation Jackson can be seen to depart from a repudiation of the state's sovereignty, on the grounds of the racism and injustices it has advanced and tolerated. Of course, there have been strategic and limited interactions with formal politics, but any relationship of dependence on the state has been avoided.

Established in 2014, Cooperation Jackson is situated within the city of Jackson in the southern US state of Mississippi. With the end of Jim Crow laws enforcing racial segregation in the 1960s, Jackson, like many other places in the United States, experienced 'white flight' from integration. The city now has a Black population of over 80 per cent, the highest for a US city. With around 150,000 inhabitants, the majority population translates into Black leadership in city hall but continued exclusion from the economy and deep inequalities between Black and white populations. Jackson is a poor city, with high levels of crime, experiencing long-term processes of shrinkage in population and economic base. The state of Mississippi, with its majority Republican, majority white state government, is hostile to the city's government and leftist inclinations, often withholding resources, blocking legislation and threatening state takeover. Few places in the United States 'can be considered less progressive than the state of Mississippi'.[34]

Within this context, Cooperation Jackson aims, in the first instance, for collective organization of and control over urban economies, democratizing the means of production.[35] The project is an organizational focal point for a movement seeking new institutional arrangements and practices embedded in urban collective life. The long-term stance it takes towards to the state appears clear – stand apart, maintain independence from oppressive institutions, and build autonomous alternatives rather than seek collaboration. The idea of establishing dual power might be seen as an attempt to tidy up and formalize the messiness of the 'state nexus' with two poles of political power.[36] Cooperation Jackson certainly sees the state as having no integral role in its project of democracy – understandably, given the state's centrality to the inequalities and injustices in Jackson and beyond. But would a closer or more frequent engagement with the state advance its cause? And what would be lost if it did engage?

Nonetheless, this idealism, what we have understood as the necessary urge of democratic claims to be apart from the state, is accompanied by flurries of strategic engagement with formal politics. Cooperation Jackson has formed alliances with mayors in the city, who have in turn committed to the general aims of the project. The best illustration of this was the understanding reached with the radical Chokwe Lumumba, who Cooperation Jackson supported to become a city council member in 2009, helped get elected as mayor in 2013, and assisted with the implementation of his participatory budgeting.[37] His death in 2014, and the mayorship of his son, Chokwe Antar Lumumba, from 2017, have led to a growing distance between Cooperation Jackson and formal politics. From this we might conclude that the project is indeed willing to engage the state, but only when it sees the conditions as conducive, and the bar is set high.

There is a strong institutionalism to this project, centred on the form of the cooperative. It is one emerging from urban collective life and directly concerned with expanding opportunities of self-government. Aiming in particular for economic autonomy and decommodification, Cooperation Jackson has experimented not only with the development of institutional networks of cooperatives in the economy, schooling, urban agriculture and housing, but also with developing other forms of collective organization such as alternative currencies and time banking. The idea of an urban network of cooperatives, community land trusts and credit unions has similarities to the Preston Model, but with the decisive difference that Cooperation Jackson is not state-centred and does not seek to centre the state. It does not directly seek to transform it either, but rather to build its own alternative to the state. Of the projects discussed here it is the one that strives for the most distance to the state, and that contrasts most starkly with the Preston Model.

The democratic distance to the state adopted by Cooperation Jackson is of course internal to the state, in terms of territory, regulatory reach and imagination. The state is always present in the calculations made by democratic movements, as it must be even when the purpose is to avoid it and offer an alternative to it. It might be questioned how far Cooperation Jackson can develop without more frequent or intense engagements with state politics. Still, it is striking the extent to which the project seeks to make space for itself in urban collective life, to delineate its own urban places, practices and publics, and to marginalize the state as well as the market, making them unnecessary for urbanites through the provision of an alternative. Its vision is based on (re)building places around alternative everyday systems, for example of food and finance, allowing for self-management and collective ownership. It promotes a democratic politics immersed in everyday life, one centred on reading and study groups, training and skill sharing, community orientation meetings, and working groups on farming and sustainability.[38] While there are clear institutional preferences within this vision, particularly for the cooperative, there is an emphasis on the multiplication and diffusion of democratic opportunities within everyday settings. While still emergent, this is a democratic project where the state recedes from view, if not from force, and self-management rather than chaos proceeds.

Barcelona en Comú: occupying and supplanting the state

Barcelona en Comú, Catalan for 'Barcelona in Common', is the coming together of a range of urban movements in a political platform. It has been in city government since 2015, winning a second election on a minority mandate in 2019. At least among urban scholars, the basic story of Barcelona en Comú is well known.[39] The platform is the epicentre of the new municipalism movement. Its 'Fearless Cities' events have brought together activists and urban politicians from around the world. Its activists have sketched out a new municipalist imaginary, locating it in the global spaces of cities, in feminizing political practices, and, perhaps most crucially from our perspective, in a transition from representative to direct democracy, shifting power from state institutions to citizens and publics. Underpinning this democratic project is a sense of the potential of the 'city' as the scale and set of spaces where everything comes together.[40]

Led by Ada Colau as mayor, Barcelona en Comú's strategy can be seen as centring on 'occupying institutions' to achieve a foothold in power structures after years of anti-austerity movements and the onset of activist fatigue.[41] It has particularly strong roots in the Platform for People Affected by Mortgages (PAH) and 15M. These movements had been extremely active in the city throughout the economic crisis in Spain from 2008 onwards. Barcelona, with over 1.5 million inhabitants within the formal city boundaries (part of an urban region with a population of around 5 million), is not only one of the key economic and touristic centres in Europe, it is also a city of inequalities and a strong tradition of political activism. Barcelona en Comú was primarily an anti-austerity movement, particularly concerned with housing inequalities. It was the most high profile of the citizen platforms in Spain that came to governmental office in 2015, and it is one of the few remaining, with many, including in Madrid, losing office in the 2019 elections.[42] In contrast to Cooperation Jackson, for Barcelona en Comú taking state power is central to its project. The distance to the state is provided by the wider movement, by the range of activists involved, who locate themselves beyond formal institutions and are highly ambivalent towards the state. This is a project of democracy focused very deliberately on the state nexus, seeking transformation of the relationships between local state institutions and urban society.

Compromises abound within this nexus, and we might understand the Barcelona en Comú project as intentionally engaging with seeming incompatibilities: representative and direct democracy, state and social movements, governmental office and neighbourhood associations, political parties and popular assemblies. This 'binary-busting'[43] approach represents the most overt acceptance of the democracy/state paradox amongst the four cases explored here. The urban state envisaged by Barcelona en Comú may be non-sovereign, but it is using state sovereign power in its attempt to get there. It seeks state power in order to transform politics away from the state. It seeks to transfer power from government to citizens. But it follows conventions, in key ways. For example, it is led by a charismatic leader whose popularity has, by and large, held a coalition together, despite charged and divisive issues like Catalan independence.[44] Furthermore, as a project of government (as well as citizen mobilization), Barcelona en Comú will always be judged at least in part by its record in office. It will have to deliver in a conventional political sense as well as in a more transformative sense.

There have certainly been achievements in terms of policy change and opening up formal government to greater participation (in ways akin to many of the projects of Latin America in the preceding decades). This was most notably the case with the development of an open source participation tool to enable citizens to participate in the Barcelona en Comú's 'Smart City' project – the development of so-called 'platform municipalism'.[45] This has been accompanied by the transfer of public buildings to local communities and by the use of state power to legislate against one of the key global corporations shaping urbanization, Airbnb, which has been refused licences for rentals in areas already dominated by short-term tourist accommodation. Barcelona en Comú has also developed local programmes for undocumented migrants outside of formal citizenship rules.[46] Such moves really do attempt to enact elements of Lefebvre's right to the city idea – that citizenship and democracy should be derived from location not laws, and that those who live in the city should be able to shape it. Barcelona en Comú has also sought to foster transnational municipalism through Solidarity Cities, a network of city governments which seeks, like Sanctuary Cities, to offer an urban response to global migration, one based on solidarity and hospitality, in opposition to nation-state policies of exclusion and hostility.

In doing this, there have been attempts to change how politics is practised, with neighbourhood assemblies and some popular assemblies apparent. A key aim has been to feminize politics with practices of cooperation and solidarity, as opposed to competition and individualism. This cultural understanding of how political decisions can be made in more collective and cooperative ways is rooted in the view that the way decisions are made can shape more democratic outcomes. This seems closely aligned to Wolin's idea that democratization is a shared set of practices, even an everyday culture of acting collectively.

Alongside this feminization of political practice, a more conventional attempt to transform representation has been apparent with the increasing number of female politicians.[47] This two-pronged approach to the feminization of politics can be seen as reflecting the essence of the entire Barcelona en Comú project in its strategic and productive positioning within the democracy/state nexus. There is a clear recognition that state institutions are both an impediment to democracy that needs to be transcended, but also at the same time a terrain on which the struggle for democracy can be staged.

The paradoxes of the democracy/state nexus are nowhere more apparent than in Barcelona, where democracy is advanced through, beyond and against the state. Indeed, the institution of the 'movement party'[48] captures this attempt to bridge formal politics with the politics of the city. The movement party is a kind of strategic tool to aid the generation of the demos, avoiding the hierarchies of the political party by forming open, networked channels of public assemblies. Importantly, Barcelona en Comú was, at least initially, able to go beyond conventional activist circles by engaging citizens throughout the city, especially in terms of housing issues.[49]

But tensions emerge from adopting positions both within the state and outside it. Being in government, particularly a minority one, leads to the familiar compromises and frustrations of the parliamentary system. A good example of this is the energy company, Barcelona Energia. In April 2017, the city council established Barcelona Energia as a new municipal energy company to drive the transition to post-carbon futures, address energy poverty and build 'energy sovereignty' for the city.[50] These aims have been frustrated by EU market liberalization and national Spanish legislation, as well as by forces within the local state. Furthermore, the project has failed to ignite widespread interest amongst urbanites, even if it is pointing towards an imaginary of a more democratic urban state.

Hence, the limits of state-based projects become apparent as scalar politics sets in and coalitions of interests collide.

For all that, Barcelona en Comú provides the most coherent and ambitious vision of a democratic project of de-centring the state, aiming for a non-sovereign politics. The emergent urban state is a complex array of positions within and beyond the conventional state, operating in the different political registers of both representative and direct democracy.

Naples: non-sovereign politics and the commons

Although overshadowed by Barcelona and other Spanish cities, the southern Italian city of Naples also offers potent examples of experimental engagements with the state.[51] In contrast to Barcelona, activists in Naples did not seek state power or office, but rather attempted to repurpose state power from its fringes or interstices, as Mauro Pinto, Luca Recano and Ugo Rossi put it.[52] As elsewhere, in the wake of the global financial crisis of 2008/9, diverse urban movements and left political parties have been resurgent in Naples, a city of around 1 million inhabitants. Activists focused on the urban crisis in a context of severe austerity, contesting national and EU policy programmes.[53] In the examples we discuss here, there has been no real attempt to formalize interactions with the state. But there have been flurries of engagement between urban publics claiming urban spaces, and conventional, if progressive, local government providing them with some opportunities to do so. Relations between urban movements and the local government, led by the mayor Luigi de Magistris, are informal and ad hoc to a certain extent, but generally supportive. In 2011 de Magistris was initially helped into power through an informal coalition of citizen committees and civil society groups.[54] But when, in 2016, the mayor established a political party in response to the vibrancy of politics in Naples, many urban movements did not join, preferring to remain at the edges, at a distance to the state. People's assemblies and urban commons projects popping up in the interstices between state and society characterize this municipalist project. Projects have focused on commoning water, environment and culture, contested regeneration projects and the impacts of the municipal debt crisis.[55]

The local state has established non-state and largely informal institutions to accommodate these municipalist practices. The main institutional forms which have emerged through the collaboration between movements and the local state have been commons projects, in the form of community occupied and managed spaces recognized by the state; popular assemblies; audit consulting bodies; and popular observatories. They represent a series of loosely institutionalized spaces in which direct and everyday forms of democracy can occur.[56] Crucially, the accommodation found between urban movements and the local state respected the movements' wish not to be embedded in formalized institutions. For example, the recognition of community-owned spaces has not been achieved through new legislation but rather by the local state either refusing to evict commoning projects from state-owned property, or intervening on their behalf when the property was privately owned. In the informal collaborations which have emerged there has been a clear scalar politics, with the local state aligning with social movements against the nation state's austerity programme.[57]

The local state has thus been transforming itself, at least around the edges, adapting to democracy as practices and publics. The aversion to fixed institutions and the formalization of movement-state relations does of course make the project appear precarious. Popular assemblies were central to the highpoint of municipalism in the mid-2010s, though they were to fade quickly. Emerging in the working-class suburb of Bagnoli and drawing on a tradition of public meetings in the area, popular assemblies flourished in opposition to a regeneration project that was being pushed through by the national government of Matteo Renzi in

2015.[58] Street protests were supported and often joined by the mayor and local authority members, who openly opposed the national government and helped delay the regeneration plans. Popular assemblies took place every two weeks in 2016 in Bagnoli, spread to other areas of the city, and often included representatives of local authorities.

While the potency of the popular assemblies has faded, other loose institutional forms have emerged. However, more conventional and fixed institutions have also been embraced, such as the Observatory on the Commons of the City of Naples, the Audit Consulting Commission on Municipal Debt, and the Popular Observatory on Bagnoli. All three share something of Keane's idea of a 'monitory democracy'[59] in that they represent attempts by citizens to force transparency on the state, to hold it to account on issues of, in this case, public finances and urban development. Such institutional strategies can be seen to be premised on an acceptance that the state can be many things at the same time – 'plural', in Cooper's terms – and that democracy can be advanced through diverse forms of engagement with the state. Overall, the examples from Naples, while quite diverse, share a non-sovereign understanding of politics and seem closest to the idea of democracy as an ongoing project of renewal, seeking neither fixed institutional form nor a correct place. The distance to the state is clear and engagements are opportunistic and strategic, never aimed at taking state power or advancing it, but turning it to the advantage of their cause.

Urban democracy with(out) the state

The main proposition in this chapter is that the relationship with the state, what we think of in terms of distances to the state, shapes the possibilities for democratic politics – its scope, forms and, perhaps, even its ultimate potential. Thus the relation of projects of democracy to the state is both a strategic question and, more than this, is constitutive of democracy itself. Involvement with the state can, depending on the political system in place, entail a presence in electoral politics and political office, or the (illegal) occupation of space, autonomous action and so on. These are, on the one hand, strategic choices, requiring the situated weighing up of how to deal with existing power structures to achieve specific aims. They indicate a mix of radical/reformist intent – the scope of the democratic claim – as well as the strategic steps employed to achieve it, the practices it will entail. But they are also ultimately formative of democratic projects, as the relation to the state shapes subjectivities, the moments when the ethos of democracy takes hold, and the places where visions of democracy are situated.

Returning to our arguments in chapters 2 and 3, we can say that the urban state looks at politics and democracy through an urban lens rather than the state lens, following an urban logic rather than the state logic of politics. Hence, in an urban democracy, the state does not vanish, but rather becomes something else. Looking across the four examples discussed here, we can discern the outlines of what an *urban* state could be. Returning to Cooper's concept that the state can be plural, the urban state can then exist within, alongside and beyond the formal state. At times, an urban state encompasses a remoulding of the state to engage in and facilitate new urban logics of democracy, as in the case of Barcelona's promotion of popular assemblies and direct forms of democracy. At other times, it shrinks the state, deferring sovereignty, and allowing collective self-government to prosper where it is claimed, as for example in Naples when property rights are not enforced in relation to occupied sites. The urban state, in this sense, creates space for and accepts distanced engagements with democratic projects because it does not see itself as the locus of democracy, but as a (crucial) part of the constellation of forces shaping urban collective life.

Nevertheless, the democracy/state nexus is complicated, and always throws up contingencies. The state, given its political authority and persisting notions of political sovereignty, continues to act as a political locus. The state attracts economic and social forces pursuing their projects; it is generative of policy and law. While these attributes in themselves have nothing substantive to do with democracy, they are impossible to ignore politically. Projects need to develop strategies, be opportunistic as well as principled, and always think creatively about how the state might advance democratic politics.[60]

There is potential in the approach of Barcelona en Comú, especially in its slaying of the sacred cows of democratic politics: refusing to choose between representation or direct democracy, seeing the potential of using the former to advance the cause of the latter. Sovereign power is both harnessed, to achieve more durable power and change, and renounced, to allow self-government to emerge. Barcelona en Comú is at once intimately close and coolly distant to the state, at least on a rhetorical level, and in terms of its overall vision of democratic politics. In practice, of course, it is also a project of government and political office, one which can easily be divorced from its wider, more ambitious agenda. By contrast, Cooperation Jackson reveals the vision of a democratic movement embedded within urban collective life, renouncing state power by both implication and design. In a context of racial capitalism and a state system in which hostile institutional scales are pushing down on the local state and the city as a whole, this project seeks to completely resituate democracy. The Preston Model is, at present, somewhat state-centred and focused on democracy as a political objective, rather than as a way of actually conducting politics. Its vision of the future state does, however, have parallels with what has been happening in Barcelona. The urban state envisaged for the future in Preston is 'partnered' with society in forms of public-public partnerships (or public commons partnerships) and a growing number of cooperatives in the fields of energy and housing, which rely on a state framework to emerge but work and make decisions independently. This remains very different to the Naples examples, where movements engage with and retreat from the local state, staying at the edges, experimenting with fluid, non-state institutions, both close in initial contact but far from the state in their everyday practices. Here, movements and the local state seem to have reached an agreement, at least for a period, that a distance to the state is necessary but that engagement with it is also required in order to succeed.

To sum up the vision of the urban state, we can return to two crucial arguments made in the book. First, in order to see the political possibilities of urbanization, we require an urban lens on politics, which de-centres the state and opens up non-sovereign forms of politics. Second, democracy cannot, in its radical forms, be contained with the state, but must rest with the demos as it locates and relocates itself. The idea of the city is the place where these two lines of arguments meet. The city is the horizon of democracy and urbanization, the main shaper of their political conditions. The state is still an important player, and may still be the main opponent of democracy to face down, or the key ally to win. But the state does not stand at the centre of democracy. It does not tower over the city.

7

The City in the Age of Urbanization

Our lack of political capacity to take control of the places we live in, to act collectively on the processes which shape our daily lives, is a democratic scandal. Democracy is often, and erroneously, thought to exist mainly in abstract rights, the written texts of constitutions, election events, the occasional grand building, a parliament or even a street protest. It is an activity which happens at a distance from most of us – in political institutions, on TV, the internet and the radio – and is carried out by other people, small sections of society. The health (or not) of democracy is, accordingly, measured in terms of the status of such political activities. Even on its own inadequate terms, this form of politics seems to be in crisis, as many prominent political analysts suggest (see Chapter 1). Key economic players have sought and gained competitive advantage over democratic systems, which often appear to have given up on addressing the democratic deficits emerging from capitalism.[1] Such analyses are as piercing as they are accurate, but we should not narrow our worries about democracy down to a concern for the fate of such institutions. Important as they may often be, democracy exists rather in the coming together of the people in forms of collective rule. To advance democratic politics, we require a fresh way of thinking about democracy, a new way of grounding and practising it. In this book we have argued that the locus for this new project of democracy can be the city in conditions of global urbanization, even if at first glance those conditions may encourage little optimism.

The failings of capitalism and the failings of democracy merge dramatically in the world's cities. It seems safe to assume that most people would not vote (if they were permitted to) for the current housing crisis, or indeed, for the multiple crises apparent in cities around the world. Inequalities are laid bare in the urban fabric, where the stark contrasts between abundance and lack of amenities for a decent life are plainly in view. Global urbanization can wreak havoc with places. In the 'booming' cities of the global south, slums are erected in the midst of upscale suburban estates (and vice versa). Throughout the deindustrialized, hollowed-out cities of the global north, gentrification processes drive the displacement of urbanites.[2] In the so-called Alpha Cities,[3] the inner cities become havens for the global elite, while the poor (and increasingly middle-income residents) are pushed to the outskirts and into precarity as housing becomes subject to global economic forces and public services and social infrastructures shrink.

It is worth pausing to consider this (involuntary, forcible) displacement of people as a democratic question. Often, such displacement is written off by politicians, planners and academics as an unavoidable part of urban development, integral to the swirl of urbanization, as the necessary if not necessarily nice outcome of market forces. But is not the capacity to choose where one lives and in what conditions a question of democracy, a matter of common concern to be grasped and acted upon collectively? This is especially the case when the properties of the place of residence also shape opportunities for social and political engagement and organization. Alongside jobs (and bank balances), there can be few better indicators of our prospects within society than where we live and in what conditions. How we end up there is the result of a confluence of factors (class, education, wealth, achievement, luck and so on), but does the very situation in which we find ourselves day-in-day-out not seem like a suitable point from which to consider our common fates, to act upon them as matters of common concern, to take control of our affairs and to consider the extent of democracy in our lives, to ask whether market forces and the interests of wealth accumulation should be permitted to sweep through our lives in such a fashion?

We are used to thinking about democracy in terms of voting rights, freedom of speech and so on, but why do we not think about our relation to the spaces and places we inhabit as being a democratic question?[4] Should we not have 'spatial rights', the right to stay put for example? In reality, unless we enjoy wealth, especially property, and privilege, we have very limited resources and capacities to intervene in our immediate surroundings. The formal politics of the state limits our democratic voice to the distanced and delegated democracy of representation, to moments, like voting, and to activities which seek to bring change indirectly: protesting, lobbying, getting the state to do what we would like it to do. We urbanites are, if we are lucky, mainly reduced to forms of 'participation', of articulating interests or needs, to planning consultations and appeals. We are rendered (im)passive to our surroundings through the complex obstacles placed in front of any attempt to collectively wrest control of them from markets and governments – a combination of their jurisdictional downgrading as a matter for planning bureaucracies and local government, and their trivialization and naturalization in many academic and media debates.[5] Ultimately, we are quite alienated from our surroundings, and seemingly helpless to do anything to control or reshape them. The intense and rapid spatial transformations of urbanization become apparent in the deep lack of resonance between the people living in urban spaces and the objects, functions and rules assembled in and through them. The relation between urbanized spaces and the urbanites living in these spaces can often be mute and defunct. How did we get into this mess? And, more importantly, how can we get out of it?

What hope the city?

We have argued in this book that a democratic project of the city provides one way to deal with the urgent problems outlined above. The 'city', we have contended, is not a democratic idea stuck in the past of sovereign city-states, but is already being practised around the world by urbanites making democratic claims to the spaces around them. This book has sought, with the help of diverse strands in the urban studies literature, to offer a vision and vocabulary for a democratic politics that delineates the horizon of this project of the city.

A crucial starting point for understanding the purchase of this democratic horizon is that the city is both an actual and a virtual place, and that political meaning emerges through the interaction of the two.[6] What does that denote? First, that the city can be a place, with a name, 'Beirut', 'Bengaluru', 'Berlin'. But such places are best seen not as jurisdictionally demarcated or fixed spatial categories, but as looser, if still distinct, locations within urbanization. They have a materiality, a social life, and sometimes strong political traditions. This socio-materiality can provide the conditions within which democracy flourishes, from everyday interactions to moments of coming together in the squares and in other places of meaning-making. This also means that the city as a lived democratic space and idea precedes its naming. The global processes through which cities and other urban spaces are shaped become visible, turn into bricks and stones, parks and recs, encounters and struggles in the actual places and sites of the city wherever it takes place.

It is here that the materiality of the city most clearly gives way to the idea of the city. Ideas about what a city means are often contested, but this reveals political productivity and scope. Furthermore, ideas about the city always exceed what is there in the materiality of the named place. The notions, hopes and projects of the city exceed the actual places in which they are articulated. It is in this sense that the city can provide a horizon of democracy. It can be the location where claims are made, a location that is both actual and material (made up of the places urbanites inhabit) and conceptual and normative (a place of ideas and values). Indeed, it is a kind of 'concrete utopia', embedded within but reaching beyond existing urban places. Sometimes urbanites do claim a right to the city as an imagined place, but in doing so they are also claiming a democratic right to the actual places they inhabit. And, vice versa, when urbanites make a claim to a specific city as a democratic place, they are also making a claim to that city as an imagined place.

That the city can offer an alternative horizon of democracy to the nation state was made very clear in Glasgow in May 2021. When immigration officers seized two men on Kenmure Street in the Pollokshields area of the city, they were soon to be surrounded by hundreds of protestors. The two men were Sumit Sehdev and Lakhvir Singh, originally from India. They were long-term residents of the city, but without the formal right to stay permanently in the UK. With the two men already in the immigration services van, protestors blocked the street, preventing passage of the vehicle. A stalemate ensued, with protestors demanding the release of the men, and the immigration officers refusing. Eventually, the police arrived and broke the stalemate by forcing the immigration officers to release the men, to huge cheers, on the grounds that the situation was a health and safety risk (all this took place during a Covid-19 lockdown).

Afterwards, Pinar Aksu, from the city's Maryhill Integration Network, said of the immigration services: 'They messed with the wrong city.'[7] In this moment she evoked an idea of a specific place, Glasgow. Now, Glasgow is one of those cities which has a strong sense of itself as a political place, with a history of collective action, protest and unruliness in solidarity, going back to 'Red Clydeside' and the Rent Strikes of the early twentieth century. This rich history specific to Glasgow offers contemporary residents an idea of the city as a political project and a place where democracy can be struggled for. But the potency of this evocation of the city lies not only in the past and the place itself, and necessarily so.

Like anywhere else, Glasgow is a contested place, with very different visions of the city practised by its residents. This was made clear by events only a few weeks later, when a refugee rally in the city centre was met by far-right protestors, violent in their claim to be 'protecting' war monuments and the like in the city's main square.[8] This illustrates why claims to a democratic city always draw on a wider normative idea of what a city should be. Such an imaginary goes beyond the actuality of a specific place, opening up possibilities and offering means to bridge diverse demands. Put differently, the democratic imaginary of the city will always exceed the materiality of the place. Indeed, it will provide an open, expansive horizon within which claims to a more democratic world can be made. In demanding the release of Sumit Sehdev and Lakhvir Singh, the protesters were also demanding, enacting even, a different city, one in which these things do not happen and where direct action of this sort can, indeed, change things.

As images and footage of the protests and the eventual release of the two men circulated on global media sites, it was hard not to feel inspired. Even if the episode did not denote a fundamental change, it was a striking example of the demos in action, of a public in *place*, of the idea of the city being mobilized and the state being both resisted and enrolled in the moment. The demos emerged within the territory of the state, and the state was forced to adapt, to comply. The demos won the day. The state in this episode presents itself as a differentiated actor: the police worked against the immigration service, if only for a moment. This touches on a crucial thread running through this book. The state need not be considered as a (monolithic) thing to be conquered or smashed. While it can be neither the agent nor the location of democracy, and is often its obstacle, the state is fluid, heterogeneous, and offers contingent possibilities for democratic projects.

The example from Glasgow does, then, encapsulate much about the potential of urban democracy as envisaged in this book. The protestors can be viewed, in the terms employed here, as an insurgent urban public, as enacting the demos. Where did they come from, how did they get there so fast, and how did they even know what was happening? It was almost like the demos sprang from the very ground of the city. Obviously, there was organization – the clicking into place of a network of activists (in this case the No Evictions Network) communicating with other activists, people speaking to each other, bodies being put on the streets. But we can assume that there was also some spontaneity in the making of this political space, that some curious residents came out of their homes to find out what was happening, and stayed because they too wanted to prevent the detention of the two men. As Pinar Aksu went on to say: 'This is a revolution of people coming together in solidarity for those who others have turned away from.'[9]

It was a great result first and foremost for Sumit Sehdev and Lakhvir Singh, and it was also a great moment for urban democracy. But it was just that – a moment. Its limits are very apparent. Sehdev and Singh still have – at the time of writing – no formal right of permanent residence. State immigration institutions have not changed, and the urban public dispersed, never again to reconvene exactly in that place and with that composition of people coming together in common cause. Urban collective life is the source of urban democratic action, and is capable of effecting change, but it can also be transient, reliant on moments and resonances of collectivity that are difficult to sustain or extend. In the final pages of the book, we review how these ambiguities have been addressed in the preceding chapters, and consider how things may be moved forward.

The political force of urban collective life

Throughout this book we have emphasized that urban democracy already exists, even if it is diverse and fragmented. When we delve into the everyday life of cities, places 'where everything comes together',[10] we can see that people are already practising democracy, albeit differently in a variety of settings and locations. The view taken here is that urban spaces – in core cities, suburban settlements or at the urban periphery – are full of diverse practices, ideas and visions of alternative politics and democracy. What we need is a way of thinking about them as a form of democracy per se. Indeed, these practices are not just proto-political acts or insurgencies; their lack of institutional form or legalistic basis is no indicator of their democratic qualities. Rather, they sketch out a different logic and terrain of political engagement and practice that are, if not entirely detached from, then at one remove from state-centred politics. This idea of democracy starts where people are actually living, in the conditions of urban life for ordinary people and not in the strategies and institutions of parties and governments – to paraphrase the *May Day Manifesto* of the New Left.[11]

The main argument of this book is easily summarized: democracy can be a transformative political project when it is (re)imagined in relation to urbanization. Democracy is, at its core, a simple idea, however difficult and divisive its realization may be. It is about the rule of the people and devising the means to achieve that rule. Wolin, from whom we have taken inspiration, stresses that democracy needs to be grounded in the life worlds of citizens: 'In my understanding, democracy is a project concerned with the political potentialities of ordinary citizens, that is with their possibilities for becoming political beings through the self-discovery of common concerns and of modes of action for realizing them.'[12]

When thinking about the merits of democracy, we should therefore begin by asking: Where are the people, the demos, in the making of cities and urbanization? Why are they only involved intermittently? Taking this simple approach to democracy, we might be able to overcome the fixation on the state so prevalent in conventional accounts.

The first step in doing this is to look at politics through the urban lens, so that the possibilities of the age of global urbanization become apparent. Our arguments might have drawn on scholarly debate, but the political centrality of urbanization is recognized increasingly widely. Take the recently established German political party, Die Urbane (the Urbanites). While we would argue that forming a(nother) political party may not be the first thing the urban conditions of politics necessitate, Die Urbane is, as far as we can tell, the only political party established on the premise that urbanization is the dominating force in our world and that, as such, we are, or should all consider ourselves, subjects of it, i.e. urbanites.

Die Urbane's website eloquently states that the 'urban' is the place where it all comes together politically, in both material and, crucially, metaphorical spaces – the urban is where the Zeitgeist is determined.[13] For Die Urbane, the urban provides a way of thinking about our world so shaped by urbanization. But it also offers a way of organizing the world collectively. We are all urbanites, they say. The implication is that we are all – regardless of which nation we live in, whether we live on a farm, in a hamlet, village, town, city or megacity – in some ways urbanites. We have something in common because urbanization shapes everywhere and everyone – it is not a process exclusive to 'urban' areas, like towns and cities. Hence, despite the challenges urbanization presents, at the same time it offers something politically productive, a potential to be grasped. It just has to be re-connected to democracy. This does not have to be read as a claim for a new urban form of the global cosmopolitanism that was so apparent in academic and political discourses in the 1990s and 2000s.[14] Our arguments here are not as prescriptive; rather, they rest on the idea that the city can provide a way to find common cause and action in a context of global urbanization.

Urbanization is generative of a different rationality of political engagement and, with that, a different democratic vision. The urban lens we detailed in Chapter 2 allowed us to see ongoing democratic struggles as driven in part by the desire to find resonance and generate self-governing capacity in relation to physical, social and political environments that have been so transformed in such uneven ways. Indeed, if we understand the city as the common property of its inhabitants, it is crucial to examine how urbanites actually relate to and inhabit these urban spaces. What can they change or do to renegotiate them? This is a question of urban democracy.

The urban meaning of democracy

Throughout the book, we have argued that how people can or cannot relate to their immediate spatial environment, and how it is used, maintained and made available, is a genuine matter of democracy. We interpret the now popular claim for a right to the city in this way. It is not about codified legal claims but rather a collective political claim to have access to, to participate in and to enjoy the benefits of urbanization as a collective project and common property. It is about the capacity to generate new spaces of urban collective life out of urbanization. But in order to appreciate the democratic character of this struggle, we need to reimagine what democracy might look like and how it is practised. To do so, we suggest three major shifts in how we perceive democracy. The emergent urban democracy we envision might best be approached through:

1) its distinct practices rather than any institutional form,
2) its entanglement with urban places and materialities instead of its jurisdictional scale, and
3) urban democratic publics which make matters of concern visible and at the same time provide the grounds for different political subjectivities.

These shifts have their roots in the radical democracy tradition and Wolin's work in particular. Following him, we considered the demos as the life force of democracy.[15] Many theorists and politicians have seen the demos as chaotic and in need of subjugation to an enlightened elite. In Wolin's view, by contrast, democracy is inconceivable without the demos at its heart, because the demos alone generates common grievances, collective identities and forms of collective rule. The problem, he argued, is that the demos is not simply there, but needs to emerge, to take shape in struggle. The demos cannot be institutionalized and confined but needs to be crafted, enacted and recurrently self-fashioned. 'The demos becomes political, not simply when it seeks to make a system of governance more responsive to its needs, but when it attempts to shape the political system in order to enable itself to emerge, to make possible a new actor, collective in nature.'[16]

The socio-materiality of urbanization, the particular places where it unfolds, offers resources for an emergent demos: the people themselves, the conditions of urban society like proximate diversity, and the shared everyday experiences of urban collective life.[17] The processes that transform the sites of encounter and engagement also impact on how people understand themselves as political subjects, how they organize themselves and the issues they pursue politically. Intense urbanization transforms the material conditions of everyday life, sociability and political embeddedness for urbanites across the globe. Yet, these conditions also provide a communicative background for political organization, shared grievances and the making of collective claims to democracy.[18] There is ultimately something that the state, or for that matter the market, cannot dominate or take away from people, however hostile and invasive the state or the market may be. This is the power of collective social action, which in this democratic project is imagined through the city. Simone and Pieterse, amongst others, have directed our focus to urban collective life as a way to comprehend how urbanization unfolds.[19] Urban collective life encompasses a variety of things, actions and agents. What is productive in urban collective life are the morphing energies of human and non-human agents, which at points of resonance become visible as situated urban publics.

It is at this point that the city as an idea of democracy becomes relevant. The city is an actual/virtual site, source and stake of democratic struggles. To reiterate, the city in this understanding is not a bounded entity or a distinct scale of political action, but a collective project which generates different types of social property, and a democratic vision of self-government on the basis of solidarity amongst strangers.

The city is a category of political practice, not of geographical analysis. The democratic project here rests on a strong sense of the contingency of the urban, a sense that stable functioning networks should not obscure their reliance on practices, alignments between people, and their socio-material environments. Recent developments in cities certainly bear witness to an increasing focus on practices – what we have called urban everyday politics.[20] These practices are often closely interlinked with other forms of politics, from social movements to neighbourhood groups, political parties and the institutions of the state. But they entail a different, an *urban*, way of being political.[21] Political experiences, affects and logics are shaped and conditioned by the urban contexts in which they are located, in the 'here and now' of urban collective life where bodies, ideas and collectives can confront urbanization.

We argue that these practices, diverse as they are, share a de-centred way of practising democracy. De-centred in two fashions. First, the practices are not bounded by a state-logic with a clear centre of authority, a hierarchy of power attached to it, and defined boundaries between spheres of individual and collective actions. Second, the spatiality of these practices cannot be readily delineated because they co-produce the democratic spaces on which they depend. They are in need of places but they do not conform to a logic of political scales. What they all share is a prefigurative momentum in that they embody the social relations they seek to enact.[22]

Further, the city as democratic imaginary helps to forge coalitions between different struggles across different fields. Indeed, urban publics are often interlinked and networked across several domains and policies. What binds them, we would argue, is the imaginary of the city as a collective project and common property apart from or at a distance to the nation state. Often the starting point for common struggles and collective organization is the feared or threatened expulsion from urban spaces and the possibilities that urbanity provides. The claim to stay put and to remain part of the city is not only a struggle against a geographical or spatial exclusion. As was shown in the diverse cases discussed in Chapter 5, it is also a struggle against economic and political exclusion and exploitation based on labour relations, and part of a wider claim to urbanity. Such struggles are really a fight against expropriation (or accumulation by dispossession) placed outside the wage nexus.[23] Urbanites co-produce the value of urbanity which preconditions the value of urban land and physical infrastructures.[24] It is often the expropriative and extractive form of urbanization and its effects that lead people to organize, claim their rights and pursue acts of citizenship. It is in this sense that a distinct urban form of democratic action can be perceived.

Moving forward

Our arguments have not rested on returning democratic politics to the 'city' of old, or resurrecting the city-state. Global urbanization has rendered notions of sovereignty and boundaries problematic. We have contended that an urban democracy can subvert the centrality of the (nation) state and assert the collective claims of (urban) society. Urban democracy as reimagined here has been about learning from ongoing activisms that find potential rather than fear in this reassembling of state-society relations. Taking inspiration from, for example, urban migrants and municipalism, we have outlined a democratic vision of collective self-rule, of finding common cause and developing collective forms of organization within the processes of urbanization.

But, of course, urban democracy does not fall from the sky like pennies from heaven. The 'city' we envisage is one that requires a different idea of being an urbanite or becoming a citizen. The sense that democracy requires an active citizenry, a sense of publicness, runs through much political theory. Wolin argues that it is the very practices of becoming visible, part of a collective, that enable and embed such a democratic culture. There is a risk of falling into the communitarian trap, i.e. conceiving of communities as the proper answer to questions of disintegration, alienation and democratic renewal. Iris Marion Young proposes 'city life', understood as 'the being together of strangers', as an 'alternative to both the ideal of community and the liberal individualism it criticizes as asocial'.[25] Urbanites interact with and experience shared urban spaces and institutions, and this can facilitate the development of a common understanding of grievances and solidarity. However, this does not lead automatically to unity or homogeneity. Even when they share places, urbanites might develop different senses of those places.[26] Hence, there is a genuine democratic tension inscribed in the idea of 'city life', between being in and sharing a common world and the heterogeneous and plural nature of this world.

The democracy detailed here is a project, one whose vitality lies in the advancement not only of a different way of doing democracy, but also of a very different understanding of being and living in (urban) space. In developing collective action, communality rests on a sense of shared urban practices in a world in transition.[27] This requires work, of course, but it is the work of urban collective life. Therein lies hope. Our delineation of the practices, publics and places of democracy has analytical purchase, but it also underlines that this form of democratic politics is all around us. Urban democracy has nowhere to go beyond urban collective life – but there is the potential for a virtuous circle here, one of self-generation and renewal.

Nonetheless, this version of democracy is demanding of people and challenging for the existing institutions and structures of democracy. It is very different from the 'spectator politics' found in many places. The proposed moving of politics closer to people's everyday lives, embedding democratic possibilities within them, has clear implications. The hope is that such a shift will be empowering; indeed, it will occur only through empowerment. But it will make demands on people's time and daily lives. It requires engagement and effort, and it has been noted that there is not always evidence that people want to take on such burdens.[28] The examples we have narrated in this book involve people displaying courage and strength but also patience and perseverance. Urban democracy, in our understanding, rests precisely on the will and capacity of urbanites. It is not a matter of expertise, but closer to what Wolin calls 'craftsmanship': learning the collective skills of citizenship, improving them, and working together with others to forge practices, places and publics of democracy. Will and capacity are, to be clear, not individually given properties, but are shaped and structured collectively in the immediate spaces and places people inhabit.

What does democratic craftsmanship mean in practical terms? In Chapter 4 we related the story of a politically ambitious housing cooperative in Zurich, Kraftwerk 1. The housing co-op was founded in the mid-1990s against the backdrop of a depoliticized landscape of cooperatives, which had largely become a policy tool for the city government and club-like entities concerned with the interests of their increasingly middle-class members. Yet, Kraftwerk 1 (along with other cooperatives in this period) realized that the organizational form of a cooperative provides a productive space in which to experiment with new forms of collective urban living, a rich source from which to develop political agency. At the same time, the history of the existing co-ops was a permanent reminder that the housing cooperative as a form does not safeguard the democratic intent and political purpose of the cooperative. Indeed, it is only through 'practising' the cooperative as a collective that the meaning of democratizing housing can be realized and interrogated. Kraftwerk 1 did this by assembling every month to discuss issues of daily life, but also to debate questions of strategic importance. There is a certain political vibrancy in its communal life, which has meant the political urgency present at the beginning of its creation has never faded. This can be seen in Kraftwerk 1's new housing projects addressing political matters of concern, such as the lack of non-profit housing and common amenities at the urban peripheries. In doing so, the cooperative has also inspired or forced other housing co-ops to develop more politically ambitious agendas. Indeed, recurrent challenges or provocations from both inside and outside seem to be vital in crafting an ethos of democratic engagement.

Our idea of urban democracy depends on spaces in which it can be practised and learned not in the abstract but in the actual material world. This provides a different starting point of engagement, one more intuitive in relation to everyday life. These spaces can be very different. As we explored in Chapter 4, the home can become a democratic space, where solidarity and collectivity around everyday grievances and (im)possibilities can be located. Housing activists have provided new forms of living and a performative critique of existing property regimes, which can be seen as a precondition for tackling them in more institutional venues. In Chapter 5 we saw how cycling through city streets could become generative of political subjectivities, as with the Critical Mass movement. We also detailed how marginalization and exclusion from the urban common-wealth can be countered by occupying space and making claims to citizenship in the city, in the global south and beyond. This urban kind of democratic politics can have many repertoires – it can be contestatory, opportunistic and so on – but it is always aimed at generating alternative futures.

It is a politics which sees no disconnect between the world on the doorstep and democratic values and hopes. It is a politics that does not revolve around the state. It might begin with making common cause with neighbours, and then with others, further away, who have experienced similar conditions. Of course, one might say that the housing problem, for instance, would be easier to address if urban land was owned by the public in the first place. But, in any case, that land was probably once owned and then sold by the state. Or, even worse, the state expropriated the land and handed it over to powerful economic interests. Why would this not be repeated in the next round of state restructuring? Public housing has been and still is a viable and effective solution. At the same time, the provision of housing by state agencies does not provide spaces of urban democracy per se. As understood here, urban democracy is always about participation and connection to the material environments that shape and mark our lives. If it is not possible to relate in this way, the simple provision of buildings will not enhance place-based attachment or reduce the lack thereof. It is not in itself democratically empowering, however many practical benefits it might have for people.

Urban democracy will always be shaped to a certain extent by existing structures, places and networks for social encounters, political organizing and visible claim-making. As detailed in Chapter 6, new municipalist projects have helped sketch out an alternative horizon of possibility in their varied attempts to work at interstitial distances to the state. We have noted the moves that have been made to realign the state and urban society in a productive tension, with the goal of resituating the demos at the heart of politics. Projects like Barcelona en Comú seek to go beyond those past democratic visions of the city we detailed in Chapter 1, municipal socialism and urban social movements. In Barcelona, the democracy/state nexus has been embraced through attempts to overcome the binaries of formal/extra-formal politics, local/global, present/future gains, and incremental versus systematic change. The new municipalist projects we detailed, especially in Naples, showed an embrace of urban publics, even in their ephemeral and fragmented quality, with the state at times seeking partnership with them in a non-sovereign politics. Both these cases underlined how the state can be plural, operating in different registers for different purposes, even if it can never be the force or host of democracy itself.

There can, then, be no singular encompassing vision

of an urban democracy and its rightful relations to the state. Just as democratic publics, practices and places are ongoing, an urban democracy is always an unpredictable project. Given the democracy/state nexus, projects that adopt interstitial distances to the state have no ideal outcomes, only approximations of what democracy can be. Urban democracy will exist only in its interactions with the state; there is no political nirvana beyond this. The specific relations between the state and urban logics of politics are key to explaining the scope of projects of democracy – their potential as well as their limits. Thus, urban democracy does not have a clear future, even if we think there is reason to be hopeful for it. This hope rests not on a singular vision of urban democracy, *the* city, but on the embrace of many possible futures, *many* cities. Contingencies will abound, but an urban democracy worthy of the name will entail people resituating political decision-making in the experiences and spaces of urban collective life.

Notes

1 Why Cities?

1 Sassen, S. 1991. *The Global City*. Princeton: Princeton University Press; Atkinson, R. 2020. *Alpha City: How London Was Captured by the Super-Rich*. London: Verso.

2 Harvey, D. 2012. *Rebel Cities: From the Right to the City to the Urban Revolution*. London: Verso; Wijburg, G., Aalbers, M. and Heeg, S. 2018. The Financialisation of Housing 2.0: Releasing Housing into the Privatised Mainstream of Capital Accumulation. *Antipode* 50(4): 1098–119.

3 Wijburg, Aalbers and Heeg, The Financialisation of Housing 2.0; Wijburg, G. and Aalbers, M.B. 2017. The Alternative Financialization of the German Housing Market. *Housing Studies* 32(7), 968–89.

4 Çinar, A. and Bender, T. (eds.) 2007. *Urban Imaginaries: Locating the Modern City*. Minneapolis: University of Minnesota Press.

5 Brown, W. 2017. *Undoing the Demos: Neoliberalism's Stealth Revolution*. New York: Zone Books.

6 Davies, W. and Gane, N. 2021. Post-Neoliberalism? An Introduction. *Theory, Culture & Society* 38(6): 3–28.

7 West, C. 2016. Goodbye, American Neoliberalism. A New Era is Here. *The Guardian*, 17 November.

8 Streeck, W. 2016. *How Will Capitalism End? Essays on a Failing System*. London: Verso; Mair, P. 2013. *Ruling the Void: The Hollowing of Western Democracy*. London:

Verso; Crouch, C. 2004. *Post-Democracy*. Cambridge: Polity.

9 Bookchin, M. 1992. *Urbanization without Cities: The Rise and Decline of Citizenship*. Montreal and New York: Black Rose Books: 1.

10 For an overview of the debate around the 'city as distinct location' vs 'urbanisation as ongoing process' see Shin, H.B. 2017. Geography: Rethinking the 'Urban' and 'Urbanisation'. In Iossifova, D., Doll, C. and Gasparatos, A. (eds.) *Defining the Urban: Interdisciplinary and Professional Perspectives*. London: Taylor & Francis.

11 Keil, R. 2018. The Empty Shell of the Planetary: Re-rooting the Urban in the Experience of the Urbanites. *Urban Geography* (39)10: 1589–602.

12 Barnes, T.J. and Sheppard, E. 2010. 'Nothing Includes Everything': Towards Engaged Pluralism in Anglophone Economic Geography. *Progress in Human Geography* 34(2): 193–214.

13 Barber, B.R. 2013. *If Mayors Ruled the World: Dysfunctional Nations, Rising Cities*. New Haven: Yale University Press.

14 Atkinson, *Alpha City*. Moulart, F., Swyngedouw, E. and Rodriquez, A. 2003. *The Globalised City: Economic Restructuring and Social Polarization in European Cities*. Oxford: Oxford University Press.

15 Harvey, *Rebel Cities*; Merrifield, A. 2014. *The New Urban Question*. London: Pluto Press; Brenner, N. (ed.) 2014. *Implosion/Explosions: Towards a Study of Planetary Urbanisation*. Berlin: Jovis; Keil, R. 2018. *Suburban Planet: Making the World Urban from the Outside In*. Cambridge: Polity; Le Galès, P. 2002. *European Cities: Social Conflicts and Governance*. Oxford: Oxford University Press; Heinelt, H. and Kübler, D. (eds.) 2005. *Metropolitan Governance: Capacity, Democracy and the Dynamics of Place*. London: Routledge.

16 Enright, T. and Rossi, U. 2018. *The Urban Political: Ambivalent Spaces of Late Neoliberalism*. Cham: Palgrave Macmillan; see also the journal special issues 'Assemblages and Critical Urban Praxis', Part One, *City* 15(2): 204–40; Part Two, *City* 15(3/4): 343–88; and 'Where Is Urban Politics?', *International Journal of Urban and Regional*

Research 38(5): 1551–643. See also Roskamm, N. 2017. *Die unbesetzte Stadt: Postfundamentalistisches Denken und das urbanistische Feld*. Basel: Birkhäuser.

17 Magnusson, W. 2011. *Politics of Urbanism: Seeing Like a City*. London: Routledge; Boudreau, J.-A. 2017. *Global Urban Politics*. Cambridge: Polity; Simone, A.M. and Pieterse, E. 2017. *New Urban Worlds: Inhabiting Dissonant Times*. Cambridge: Polity; Brenner (ed.), *Implosion/ Explosions*; Robinson, J. 2006. *Ordinary Cities: Between Modernity and Development*. London: Routledge.

18 Strauss, K. 2009. Accumulation and Dispossession: Lifting the Veil on the Subprime Mortgage Crisis. *Antipode* 14(1): 10–14; Smith, N. 1996. *The New Urban Frontier: Gentrification and the Revanchist City*. New York: Routledge; Karaman, O. 2014. Resisting Urban Renewal in Istanbul. *Urban Geography* 35(2): 290–310; Aalbers, M. 2016. *The Financialization of Housing: A Political Economy Approach*. London: Routledge.

19 Barnett, C. 2014. What Do Cities Have to Do with Democracy? *International Journal of Urban and Regional Research* 38(1): 1625–43.

20 Gandy, M. and Jasper, S. (eds.) 2020. *The Botanical City*. Berlin: Jovis.

21 Wachsmuth, D. 2014. City as Ideology: Reconciling the Explosion of the City Form with the Tenacity of the City Concept. *Environment and Planning D: Society and Space* 31: 75–90; Madden, D.J. 2012. City Becoming World: Nancy, Lefebvre, and the Global-Urban Imagination. *Environment and Planning D: Society and Space* 30: 772–87.

22 Robinson, *Ordinary Cities*; Roy, A. 2016. What is Urban about Critical Urban Theory? *Urban Geography* 37(6): 810–23; Simone and Pieterse, *New Urban Worlds*.

23 Wachsmuth, City as Ideology: 77.

24 Bhan, G. 2019. Notes on the Southern Urban Practice. *Environment & Urbanization* 31(2): 639–54.

25 Angelo, H. 2017. From the City Lens Toward Urbanisation as a Way of Seeing: Country/City Binaries on an Urbanizing Planet. *Urban Studies* 54(1): 158–78; Brenner, N. and C. Schmid 2015. Towards a New Epistemology of the Urban? *City* 19(2/3): 151–82; Davidson, M. and Iveson, K.

2015. Beyond City Limits: A Conceptual and Political Defense of 'the City' as an Anchoring Concept for Critical Urban Theory. *City* 19(5): 646–64.

26 Keil, *Suburban Planet*: 189; Phelps, N.A. 2015. *Sequel to Suburbia: Glimpses of America's Post-Suburban Future*. Cambridge, MA: MIT Press.

27 Russell, B. 2019. Beyond the Local Trap: New Municipalism and the Rise of the Fearless Cities. *Antipode* 51(3): 989–1010; Thompson, M. 2021. What's New about New Municipalism? *Progress in Human Geography* 45(2): 317–42.

28 Holston, J. 2007. *Insurgent Citizenship: Disjunctions of Democracy and Modernity in Brazil*. Princeton: Princeton University Press; Beveridge, R. and Koch, P. 2019. Urban Everyday Politics: Politicising Practices and the Transformation of the Here and Now. *Environment and Planning D: Society and Space* 37(1): 142–57.

29 Euben, P.J. 2001. The Polis, Globalization, and the Politics of Place. In Botwinick A. and Connolly, W.E. (eds.) *Democracy and Vision: Sheldon Wolin and the Vicissitudes of the Political*. Princeton: Princeton University Press: 284.

30 With the term 'concrete utopia' we refer to Henri Lefebvre's and Erich Bloch's work on utopian thinking, see Levitas, R. 1990. Ernst Bloch on Abstract and Concrete Utopia. *Utopian Studies* 1(2): 13–26; Pinder, D. 2015. Reconstituting the Possible: Lefebvre, Utopia and the Urban Question. *International Journal of Urban and Regional Research* 39(1): 28–45.

31 Magnusson, *Politics of Urbanism*; Boudreau, *Global Urban Politics*; Simone, A.M. 2019. *Improvised Lives: Rhythms of Endurance in an Urban South*. Cambridge: Polity.

32 Magnusson, W. 2015. *Local Self-Government and the Right to the City*. Ithaca: McGill-Queen's University Press.

33 Barnett, What Do Cities Have to Do with Democracy?; Magnusson, W. 2014. The Symbiosis of the Urban and the Political. *International Journal of Urban and Regional Research* 38(5): 1565–71.

34 Tormey, S. 2015. *The End of Representative Politics*. Cambridge: Polity.

35 Manow, P. 2020. *(Ent-)Demokratisierung der Demokratie*. Frankfurt a.M.: Suhrkamp.; della Porta, D. 2020. *How*

Social Movements Can Save Democracy: Democratic Innovations from Below. Cambridge: Polity.

36 This is a key argument in many strands of radical democracy. See Tønder, L. and Thomassen, L. 2005. Rethinking Radical Democracy between Abundance and Lack. In Tønder, L. and Thomassen, L. (eds.) *Radical Democracy: Politics between Abundance and Lack*. Manchester: Manchester University Press.

37 Marchart, O. 2007. *Post-Foundational Political Thought: Political Difference in Nancy, Lefort, Badiou and Laclau*. Edinburgh: Edinburgh University Press; Mouffe, C. 2000. *The Democratic Paradox*. London: Verso; Butler, J. 2016. *Notes Toward a Performative Theory of Assembly*. Cambridge, MA: Harvard University Press; Wolin, S.S. 2016. *Fugitive Democracy: and Other Essays*. Edited by Nicholas Xenos. Princeton: Princeton University Press.

38 Wolin, *Fugitive Democracy*: 261.

39 Massey, D. 2008. A Global Sense of Place. In Oakes, T. and Price, P.L. (eds.) *The Cultural Geography Reader*. London: Routledge.

40 Lefebvre, H. 1991. *The Production of Space*. Oxford: Blackwell; Purcell, M. 2022. Theorising Democratic Space with and beyond Henri Lefebvre. *Urban Studies*, DOI: 10.1177/00420980211067915.

41 Baiocchi, G. 2018. *We, the Sovereign*. Cambridge: Polity.

42 Russell, Beyond the Local Trap; Thompson, What's New about New Municipalism?

43 Thompson, What's New about New Municipalism?

44 Magnusson, M. 1996. *The Search for Political Space: Globalization, Social Movements and the Urban Political Experience*. Toronto: Toronto University Press; Dogliani, P. 2002. European Municipalism in the First Half of the Twentieth Century: The Socialist Network. *Contemporary European History* 11(4): 573–96.

45 Blau, E. 1999. *The Architecture of Red Vienna, 1919–1934*. Cambridge, MA: MIT Press.

46 Kohn, M. 2003. *Radical Space: Building the House of the People*. Ithaca: Cornell University Press.

47 Dogliani, European Municipalism in the First Half of the Twentieth Century: 574.

48 Leopold, E. and McDonald, D. 2012. Municipal Socialism Then and Now: Some Lessons for the Global South. *Third World Quarterly* 33(10): 1837–53.

49 Moss, T. 2020. *Remaking Berlin: A History of the City through Infrastructure, 1920–2020*. Cambridge, MA: MIT Press: 62.

50 Magnusson, *The Search for Political Space*: 166.

51 Heindl, G. 2020. *Stadtkonflikte: radikale Demokratie in Architektur und Stadtplanung*. Wien/Berlin: Mandelbaum; Blau, *The Architecture of Red Vienna*.

52 For a discussion of municipal politics in modern London, see Hatherley, O. 2020. *Red Metropolis*. London: Repeater Books.

53 On the 'modern infrastructural ideal', see Graham S. and Marvin S. 2003. *Splintering Urbanism, Networked Services, Technological Mobilities, and the Urban Condition*. London: Routledge.

54 Harvey, *Rebel Cities*. Brenner, N. 2001. State Theory in the Political Conjuncture: Henri Lefebvre's 'Comments on a New State Form'. *Antipode* 33(5): 783–808.

55 Castells, M. 1983. *The City and the Grassroots*. London: Edward Arnold; Mayer, M. 2013. First World Urban Activism. *City* 17(1): 5–19; Roy, What is Urban about Critical Urban Theory?

56 Magnusson, *The Search for Political Space*.

57 Ibid.

58 Ibid.: 131.

59 Le Galès, P. 2021. The Rise of Local Politics. *Annual Review of Political Science* 24: 1–19.

60 Kohn, M. 2016. *The Death and Life of the Urban Commonwealth*. New York: Oxford University Press.

61 Baiocchi, *We, the Sovereign*.

62 Massey, D. 2007. *World City*. Cambridge: Polity.

63 Tonkiss, F. 2014. *Cities by Design: The Social Life of Urban Form*. Cambridge: Polity.

64 Keil, *Suburban Planet*; Rossi, U. 2017. *Cities in Global Capitalism*. Cambridge: Polity.

65 Beveridge, R. and Koch, P. 2019. Depoliticization of Urban Politics: Moving Beyond the 'Post-Political' City. In Buller, J. et al. *Comparing Strategies of (De)Politicisation in Europe*. Cham: Palgrave Macmillan.

66 Holston, J. 2009. *Insurgent Citizenship: Disjunctions of Democracy and Modernity in Brazil*. Princeton: Princeton University Press.

2 Politics through an Urban Lens

1 Acuto, M. et al. 2020. Seeing COVID-19 through an Urban Lens. *Nature Sustainability* 3: 977–8.
2 Bhan, G. et al. 2020. The Pandemic, Southern Urbanisms and Collective Life. *Society & Space*, 3 August, at https://www.societyandspace.org/articles/the-pandemic-southern-urbanisms-and-collective-life.
3 Ibid.
4 Amin, A. and Thrift, N. 2017. *Seeing Like a City*. Cambridge: Polity.
5 Kaufmann, D. and Sidney, M. 2020. Toward an Urban Policy Analysis: Incorporating Participation, Multilevel Governance, and 'Seeing Like a City'. *PS: Political Science & Politics* 53(1): 1–5.
6 Oxford English Dictionary, at https://www.lexico.com/definition/politics.
7 Tormey, *The End of Representative Politics*.
8 Ibid.
9 Magnusson, *Politics of Urbanism*; Scott, J.C. 1998. *Seeing Like a State: How Certain Schemes to Improve the Human Condition Have Failed*. New Haven: Yale University Press. See also in the same vein: Amin and Thrift, *Seeing Like a City*.
10 Graeber, D. and Wengrow, D. 2021. *The Dawn of Everything: A New History of Humanity*. New York: Farrar, Straus and Giroux.
11 Ibid.
12 Beveridge, R. and Featherstone, D. 2021. Introduction: Anti-Politics, Austerity and Spaces of Politicisation. *Environment and Planning C: Space and Politics* 39(3): 437–50.
13 Magnusson, W. 2010. The Puzzle of the Political. In Magnusson, W. and Shaw, K. (eds.) *A Political Space: Reading the Global Through Clayoquot Sound*. Minnesota: University of Minnesota Press: 1–2.
14 Ibid.: 2.

15 Hay, C. 2007. *Why We Hate Politics*. Cambridge: Polity: 77.
16 Magnusson, *Local Self-Government and the Right to the City*: 199.
17 Lasswell, H. 1950. *Politics: Who Gets What, When, How*. New York: Peter Smith.
18 Lukes, S. 2021. *Power: A Radical View*. London: Palgrave Macmillan.
19 Schattschneider E. 1975. *The Semi-Sovereign People: A Realist's View of Democracy in America*. Hinsdale, IL: Dryden Press.
20 Aristotle. 1992. *The Politics*. London: Penguin.
21 Marchart, O. 2019. *Post-Foundational Theories of Democracy: Reclaiming Freedom, Equality, Solidarity*. Edinburgh: Edinburgh University Press.
22 Featherstone, D. 2012. *Solidarity: Hidden Histories and Geographies of Internationalism*. London: Zed Books.
23 Magnusson, The Symbiosis of the Urban and the Political: 1571.
24 E.g. Magnusson, *Politics of Urbanism*; Scott, *Seeing Like a State*.
25 Magnusson, The Symbiosis of the Urban and the Political: 1563.
26 Cochrane, A. 2007. *Understanding Urban Policy: A Critical Approach*. Oxford: Blackwell.
27 Allen, J. and Cochrane, A. 2014. The Urban Unbound: London's Politics and the 2012 Olympic Games. *International Journal of Urban and Regional Research* 38(5): 1609–24; McCann, E. and Ward, K. (eds.) 2011. *Mobile Urbanism: Cities and Policymaking in the Global Age*. Minneapolis: University of Minnesota Press; Peck, J. and Theodore, N. 2015. *Fast Policy: Experimental Statecraft at the Threshold of Neoliberalism*. Minneapolis: University of Minnesota Press.
28 For an overview see Davies, J.S. and Imbroscio, D.L. (eds.) 2009. *Theories of Urban Politics*. Los Angeles: Sage; Davidson, M. and Martin, D. (eds.) 2014. *Urban Politics: Critical Approaches*. Los Angeles: Sage; John, P., Mossberger, K. and Clarke, S.E. 2012. *The Oxford Handbook of Urban Politics*. Oxford: Oxford University Press.

29 John, P. 2009. Why Study *Urban* Politics? In Davies and Imbroscio (eds.) *Theories of Urban Politics*: 21.
30 Dahl, R.A. 1961. *Who Governs? Democracy and Power in an American City*. New Haven: Yale University Press; Hunter, F. 1953. *Community Power Structure: A Study of Decision Makers*. Chapel Hill: University of North Carolina Press.
31 Riordan, W. 1963. *Plunkitt of Tammany Hall: A Series of Plain Talks on Very Practical Politics*. New York: E.P. Dutton; Caro, R. 1975. *The Power Broker: Robert Moses and the Fall of New York*. New York: Vintage.
32 See for a critique of the urban regime paradigm: Jones-Correa, M. and Wong, D. 2015. Whose Politics? Reflections on Clarence Stone's Regime Politics. *Urban Affairs Review* 51(1): 161–70.
33 Peterson, P. 1981. *City Limits*. Chicago: University of Chicago Press.
34 On Berlin in the 1990s see Beveridge, R. 2011. *A Politics of Inevitability: The Privatisation of the Berlin Water Company, the Global City Discourse and Governance in 1990s Berlin*. Wiesbaden: VS Springer.
35 Peters, B.G. and Pierre, J. 2012. Urban Governance. In John, Mossberger and Clarke (eds.) *The Oxford Handbook of Urban Politics*: 72.
36 Logan, J.R. and Molotch, H.L. 1987. *Urban Fortunes: The Political Economy of Place*. Berkeley: University of California Press; Stone, C.N. 1989. *Regime Politics: Governing Atlanta, 1946–1988*. Lawrence: University Press of Kansas; Pierre, J. 2011. *The Politics of Urban Governance*. New York: Palgrave Macmillan; Davies and Imbroscio (eds.) *Theories of Urban Politics*.
37 Davies, J.S. 2021. *Between Realism and Revolt: Governing Cities in the Crisis of Neoliberal Globalism*. Bristol: Bristol University Press.
38 Castells, M. 1977. *The Urban Question: A Marxist Approach*. Cambridge, MA: MIT Press; Castells, M. 1978. *City, Class and Power*. London: Macmillan; Castells, M. 1983. *The City and the Grassroots: A Cross-Cultural Theory of Urban Social Movements*. London: Edward Arnold.
39 Roy, What is Urban about Critical Urban Theory?; Merrifield, *The New Urban Question*.

40 Shaw, K. 2015. The Intelligent Woman's Guide to the Urban Question. *City* 19(6): 781–800; Mayer, M. 2013. First World Urban Activism: Beyond Austerity Urbanism and Creative City Politics. *City* 17(1): 5–19.
41 Lefebvre, *The Production of Space*.
42 Merrifield, *The New Urban Question*: 15–16.
43 Simone and Pieterse, *New Urban Worlds*.
44 Amin and Thrift, *Seeing Like a City*.
45 Magnusson, The Symbiosis of the Urban and the Political: 1561.
46 Brenner and Schmid, Towards a New Epistemology of the Urban?: 178.
47 Boudreau, *Global Urban Politics*.
48 Ibid.: 171.
49 Ibid.: 13.
50 Ibid.: 16; 60.
51 Lefebvre, H. 2002. *Critique of Everyday Life*. London: Verso.
52 Lefebvre, H. 1976. *The Survival of Capitalism*. London: Allen and Busby: 89.
53 Roberts, J. 2006. *Philosophizing the Everyday*. London: Pluto Press; Beveridge and Koch, Urban Everyday Politics.
54 This literature challenges the universalism that underpins much of the urban studies field and the dominance of the global north as a producer of knowledge and exemplifier of urbanism. See Robinson, *Ordinary Cities*; Sheppard, E., Leitner, H. and Maringanti, A. 2013. Provincializing Global Urbanism: A Manifesto. *Urban Geography* 34(7): 893–900; Roy, A. 2009. The 21st Century Metropolis: New Geographies of Theory. *Regional Studies* 43(6): 819–30; Derickson, K.D. 2018. Urban Geography III: Anthropocene Urbanism. *Progress in Human Geography* 42(3): 425–35.
55 Roy, What is Urban about Critical Urban Theory?: 810.
56 Bayat, A. 2010. *Life as Politics: How Ordinary People Change the Middle East*. Stanford: Stanford University Press.
57 Hentschel, C. 2015. Postcolonializing Berlin and the Fabrication of the Urban. *International Journal of Urban and Regional Research* 39(1): 79–91.

58 Vasudevan, A. 2015. The Makeshift City: Towards a Global Geography of Squatting. *Progress in Human Geography* 39(3): 316–37.
59 Brenner and Schmid, Towards a New Epistemology of the Urban?: 177.
60 Beveridge and Koch, Urban Everyday Politics.
61 Ibid.; cf. Allen and Cochrane, The Urban Unbound.
62 Amin and Thrift, *Seeing Like a City*.
63 Wachsmuth, City as Ideology; Madden, City Becoming World; Davidson and Iveson, Beyond City Limits.
64 Crouch, *Post-Democracy*; Hay, *Why We Hate Politics*.
65 Swyngedouw, E. 2007. Impossible/Undesirable Sustainability and the Post-Political Condition. In Krueger, J.R. and Gibbs, D. (eds.) *The Sustainable Development Paradox*. New York: Guilford Press: 13–40; Swyngedouw, E. 2009. The Antinomies of the Postpolitical City: In Search of a Democratic Politics of Environmental Production. *International Journal of Urban and Regional Research* 33(3): 601–20.
66 Swyngedouw, The Antinomies of the Postpolitical City.
67 MacLeod, G. 2011. Urban Politics Reconsidered: Growth Machine to Post-democratic City? *Urban Studies* 48(12): 2629–60; Beveridge, R. and Koch, P. 2017. The Post-Political Trap? Reflections on Politics, Agency and the City. *Urban Studies* 54(1): 31–43; Beveridge, R. and Koch, P. 2017. What Is (Still) Political about the City? *Urban Studies* 54(1): 62–6.
68 Rodgers, S., Barnett, C. and Cochrane, A. 2014. Where is Urban Politics?. *International Journal of Urban and Regional Research* 38(5): 1551–60; Davidson and Iveson, Beyond City Limits; Mitchell, D., Attoh, K. and Staeheli, L. 2015. Whose City? What Politics? Contentious and Non-contentious Spaces on Colorado's Front Range. *Urban Studies* 52(14): 2633–48; McFarlane, C. 2016. The Geographies of Urban Density: Topology, Politics and the City. *Progress in Human Geography* 40(5): 629–48; Phelps, *Sequel to Suburbia*.
69 Rickards, L., Gleeson, B., Boyle, M. and O'Callaghan, C. 2016. Urban Studies after the Age of the City. *Urban Studies* 53(8): 1525.

70 Merrifield, A. 2013. The Urban Question under Planetary Urbanisation. *International Journal of Urban and Regional Research* 37: 909–22; Brenner and Schmid, Towards a New Epistemology of the Urban?
71 Scott, A.J. and Storper, M. 2015. The Nature of Cities: The Scope and Limits of Urban Theory. *International Journal of Urban and Regional Research* 39(1): 12.
72 Beveridge and Koch, What Is (Still) Political about the City?
73 Khatam, A. and Haas, O. 2018. Interrupting Planetary Urbanisation: A View from Middle Eastern Cities. *Environment and Planning D: Society and Space* 36(3): 439–55.
74 Keil, The Empty Shell of the Planetary.
75 Beveridge and Koch, Urban Everyday Politics.
76 Imbroscio, D. L. 2010. *Urban America Reconsidered.* Ithaca: Cornell University Press.
77 See here in particular: Beveridge and Koch, Urban Everyday Politics.
78 Wright, E.O. 2010. *Envisioning Real Utopias.* London: Verso.

3 Democracy and the City Reimagined

1 Kohn, *Urban Commonwealth*; Magnusson, *Local Self-Government and the Right to the City*: 281ff.; Marchart, O. 2010. *Die politische Differenz: zum Denken des Politischen bei Nancy, Lefort, Badiou, Laclau und Agamben.* Berlin: Suhrkamp: 329ff.; Rosa, H. 2021. *Resonance: A Sociology of Our Relationship to the World.* Cambridge: Polity.
2 Marchart, *Post-Foundational Political Thought.*
3 See Euben, The Polis, Globalization, and the Politics of Place: 256–90.
4 Wolin, *Fugitive Democracy*: 98.
5 Ibid.: 99.
6 Brown, W. 2010. We Are All Democrats Now .... *Theory & Event* 13(2).
7 Howarth, D.R. 2008. Ethos, Agonism and Populism: William Connolly and the Case for Radical Democracy. *The British Journal of Politics and International Relations* 10(2): 171–93; Wenman, M. 2013. *Agonistic Democracy:*

Constituent Power in the Era of Globalisation. Cambridge: Cambridge University Press; Tønder and Thomassen (eds.), *Radical Democracy*; Laclau and Mouffe, *Hegemony and Socialist Strategy*; Comtesse, D., Flügel-Martinsen, O., Martinsen, F. and Nonhoff, M. (eds.) 2019. *Radikale Demokratietheorie: ein Handbuch*. Berlin: Suhrkamp.

8 Marchart, *Post-Foundational Political Thought*; Nancy, J-L. 2010. *The Truth of Democracy*. New York: Fordham University Press; Rancière, J. 1999. *Disagreement: Politics and Philosophy*. Minneapolis: University of Minnesota Press; Balibar, É. 2014. *Equaliberty: Political Essays*. Durham, NC: Duke University Press.

9 Laclau and Mouffe, *Hegemony and Socialist Strategy*.

10 Marchart, *Post-Foundational Political Thought*.

11 Honig, B. 2007. Between Decision and Deliberation: Political Paradox in Democratic Theory. *American Political Science Review* 101(1): 5.

12 Beveridge and Koch, The Post-Political Trap?; Purcell, Theorising Democratic Space with and beyond Henri Lefebvre.

13 We take the distinction between an associative and a dissociative tradition from Marchart's work on post-foundational theories of democracy. He situates the associative strand in the tradition of Arendt and the dissociative strand in the work of Carl Schmitt.

14 Wolin, *Fugitive Democracy*: 261.

15 Wolin, S.S. 1994. 'Fugitive Democracy', *Constellations* 1(1): 11–25.

16 Wolin, S.S. 1994. Norm and Form. In Euben, J.P., Wallach, J.R. and Ober, J. (eds.) *Athenian Political Thought and the Reconstruction of American Democracy*. Ithaca: Cornell University Press: 54–5; see also Kateb, G. 2001. Wolin as a Critic of Democracy. In Botwinick, A. and William E.C. (eds.) *Democracy and Vision: Sheldon Wolin and the Vicissitudes of the Political*. Princeton: Princeton University Press.

17 McIvor, D.W. 2016. The Conscience of a Fugitive: Sheldon Wolin and the Prospects for Radical Democracy. *New Political Science* 38(3): 412–13.

18 Wolin, S.S. 1981. Editorial: Why Democracy? *democracy* 1(1): 3.

19 Wolin, S.S. 1983. Editorial. *democracy* 3(4): 2.
20 Butler, J. 2012. Bodies in Alliance and the Politics of the Street. In McLagan, M. and McKee, Y. (eds.) *Sensible Politics: The Visual Culture of Nongovernmental Activism*. New York: Zone Books.
21 Reckwitz, A. 2002. Toward a Theory of Social Practices: A Development in Culturalist Theorizing. *European Journal of Social Theory* 5(2): 255–6.
22 Taylor, A. 2019. *Democracy May Not Exist, But We'll Miss It When It's Gone*. London: Verso.
23 Wolin, *Fugitive Democracy*: 377.
24 Ibid.
25 Wolin, Editorial: 5.
26 See, for instance, Magnusson, *Local Self-Government and the Right to the City*.
27 Magnusson, *Politics of Urbanism*.
28 Lefebvre, H. 1996. *Writings on Cities*. Selected, translated and introduced by Kofman, E. and Lebas, E. Oxford: Blackwell; Kohn, *Urban Commonwealth*: 179–85; Wachsmuth, City as Ideology.
29 Davidson and Iveson, Beyond City Limits.
30 Brenner (ed.), *Implosion/Explosions*.
31 Isin E.F. 2007. City.State: Critique of Scalar Thought. *Citizenship Studies* 11(2): 212.
32 Euben, The Polis, Globalization, and the Politics of Place.
33 Farías, I. 2011. The Politics of Urban Assemblage. *City* 15(3/4): 365–74; Sendra, P. and Sennett, R. 2020. *Designing Disorder: Experiments and Disruptions in the City*. London: Verso.
34 Butler, *Notes Toward a Performative Theory of Assembly*.
35 See Mueller, J.-W. 2019. What Spaces Does Democracy Need? *Soundings* 102(2/3): 203–16.
36 Dreier P., Mollenkopf, J. and Swanstrom, T. 2001. *Place Matters: Metropolitics for the Twenty-First Century*. Lawrence: University Press of Kansas.
37 Holston, J. and Appadurai, A. 1996. Cities and Citizenship. *Public Culture* 8: 187–204.
38 Derickson, K. 2018. Masters of the Universe. *Environment and Planning D: Society and Space* 36(3): 556–62; Oswin, N. 2018. Planetary Urbanization: A View from

Outside. *Environment and Planning D: Society and Space* 36(3): 540–6.

39 Kohn, *Urban Commonwealth*.

40 Kohn, *Urban Commonwealth*: 191. See also Dellenbaugh, M., Kip, M., Bieniok, M., Müller, A. and Schwegmann, M. (eds.) 2015. *Urban Commons: Moving Beyond State and Market*. Basel: Birkhäuser.

41 Ibid.

42 Holston, J. 2019. Metropolitan Rebellions and the Politics of Commoning the City. *Anthropological Theory* 19(1): 120–42.

43 Young, I.M. 2011. *Justice and the Politics of Difference*. Princeton: Princeton University Press: 237.

44 Isin, City.State: Critique of Scalar Thought: 212.

45 Brown, *Undoing the Demos*: 207.

46 Ibid.: 209.

47 Kohn, *Urban Commonwealth*: 159ff.

48 Kohn, Author Response: 934.

49 Ibid.: 935.

50 Brown, *Undoing the Demos*: 205.

51 Ibid.: 203.

52 Ibid.

53 Abensour, M. 2011. *Democracy against the State: Marx and the Machiavellian Moment*. Cambridge: Polity; Swyngedouw, E. 2020. From Disruption to Transformation: Politicisation at a Distance from the State. *Antipode* 53(2): 486–96.

54 Critchley, S. 2005. True Democracy: Marx, Political Subjectivity and Anarchic Meta-Politics. In Tønder and Thomassen (eds.), *Radical Democracy*.

55 Ibid.: 228–9.

56 Ibid.: 226.

57 See Beveridge and Koch, The Post-Political Trap?

4 Self-governing Urbanization

1 Kohn, *Urban Commonwealth*; Magnusson, *Local Self-Government and the Right to the City*.

2 See https://juch.zureich.rip/wp-content/uploads/2020/03/MenschenInBaracken.pdf.

3 Magnusson, *Local Self-Government and the Right to the City*: 172.
4 Blunt, A. and Dowling, R. 2006. *Home*. London: Routledge: 2.
5 Vilenica, A. et al. 2020. Covid-19 and Housing Struggles: The (Re)makings of Austerity, Disaster Capitalism, and the No Return to Normal. *Radical Housing Journal* 2(1): 9–28.
6 As Gareth Millington notes, referring to the work of bell hooks, 1990. *Yearning: Race, Gender, and Cultural Politics*. Boston: South End Press; see Millington, G. 2020. Public Housing and the Right to the City, *Public Books Magazine*, 26 October, at https://www.publicbooks.org/public-housing-and-the-right-to-the-city/?utm_content=buffer07fe7&utm_medium=social&utm_source=twitter.com&utm_campaign=buffer#fnref-39212-8. See also hooks, b. and West, C. 1991. *Breaking Bread: Insurgent Black Intellectual Life*. Boston: South End Press.
7 Madden, D. and Marcuse, P. 2016. *In Defense of Housing*. London: Verso.
8 Lancione, M. 2019. Radical Housing: On the Politics of Dwelling as Difference. *International Journal of Housing Policy* 20(2): 273–89.
9 Vilenica et al. Covid-19 and Housing Struggles.
10 Madden and Marcuse, *In Defense of Housing*.
11 Lancione, Radical Housing: 3.
12 Broughton, J. 2018. *Municipal Dreams: The Rise and Fall of Council Housing*. London: Verso.
13 Blomley, N. 2004. *Unsettling the City: Urban Land and the Politics of Property*. New York: Routledge; Roy, A. 2020. Emergency Urbanism. *Public Books Magazine*, Symposium on Crisis Cities, 24 November, at https://www.publicbooks.org/emergency-urbanism; Roy, A. 2017. Dis/possessive Collectivism: Property and Personhood at City's End. *Geoforum* 80, A1–A11.
14 Roy, Dis/possessive Collectivism: A7.
15 Loick, D. 2016. *Der Missbrauch des Eigentums* (The Abuse of Property). Berlin: August Verlag.
16 Hilbrandt, H. 2021. *Housing in the Margins: Negotiating Urban Formalities in Berlin's Allotment Gardens*. Hoboken: Wiley-Blackwell.

17 Lancione, Radical Housing.
18 Desmond, M. 2016. *Evicted: Poverty and Profit in the American City*. New York: Broadway Books; Pohl, L., Genz, C., Helbrecht, I. and Dobrusskin, J. 2020. Need for Shelter, Demand for Housing, Desire for Home: A Psychoanalytic Reading of Home-Making in Vancouver. *Housing Studies*, DOI: 10.1080/02673037.2020.1857708.
19 Vasudevan, A. 2017. *The Autonomous City: A History of Urban Squatting*. London: Verso.
20 Anon. 2004. *Wohlgroth*. Zürich: Edition Patrick Frey.
21 Simone and Pieterse, *New Urban Worlds*; Rosa, *Resonance*.
22 On homeownership, democracy and the financial crisis in Portugal, see Drago, A. 2017. Is This What the Democratic City Looks Like? Local Democracy, Housing Rights and Homeownership in the Portuguese Context. *International Journal of Urban and Regional Research* 41 (3): 426–42.
23 Garcìa-Lamarca, M. 2017. Creating Political Subjects: Collective Knowledge and Action to Enact Housing Rights in Spain. *Community Development Journal* 52(3): 425.
24 Wolin, *Fugitive Democracy*: 100.
25 Blanco, I., Salazar, Y. and Bianchi, I. 2020. Urban Governance and Political Change under a Radical Left Government: The Case of Barcelona. *Journal of Urban Affairs* 42(1): 18–38; Della Porta, D. et al. 2017. *Movement Party against Austerity*. Cambridge: Polity.
26 Minuchin, L. 2016. The Politics of Construction: Towards a Theory of Material Articulations. *Environment and Planning D: Society and Space* 34(5): 895–913; Minuchin, L. 2021. Prefigurative Urbanisation: Politics through Infrastructural Repertoires in Guayaquil. *Political Geography* 85: 102316.
27 It is also in this regard that the legacy of John F.C. Turner and the community architects are of great interest. See Turner, J.F.C. 1977. *Housing by People: Towards Autonomy in Building Environments*. New York: Pantheon Books. Ward, C. 1974. *Tenants Take Over*. London: Architectural Press; Towers, G. 1995. *Building Democracy: Community Architecture in the Inner City*. London: UCL Press.
28 Isaac, J.C. 1994. Oases in the Desert: Hannah Arendt on Democratic Politics. *American Political Science Review* 88(1): 156–68.

29 On the case of Zurich and the comparison with Montevideo/Uruguay, see Barenstein Duyne, J. et al. 2021. Struggles for the Decommodification of Housing: The Politics of Housing Cooperatives in Uruguay and Switzerland. *Housing Studies*, DOI: 10.1080/026730307.2021.1966392.

30 The name Ssenter for Applied Urbanism is given to form the acronym SAU, which means pig in German. Members of the SAU initiated the International Network for Urban Research and Action (INURA) in 1991, which is still operating and has some eminent members.

31 Blum, M., Hofer, A. and P.M. 1993. *KraftWerk 1: Projekt für das Sulzer-Escher Wyss Areal*. Zürich: Paranoia-City.

32 Wirz, A. 2019. Teilt alles und spielt fair. Die neuen Schweizer Wohnbaugenossenschaften und die Wohnungsfrage. *Dérive* 77: 7.

33 Ibid.

34 See, for the case of Liverpool, Thompson, M. 2021. *Reconstructing Public Housing: Liverpool's Hidden History of Collective Alternatives*. Liverpool: Liverpool University Press.

35 Hofer, A. 2001. Ein besseres Stück Stadt. *Tec21* 42: 8.

36 Beveridge, R. and Koch, P. 2021. Contesting Austerity, De-centring the State: Anti-Politics and the Political Horizon of the Urban. *Environment and Planning C: Politics and Space* 39(3): 451–68.

37 Krätke, S. 2004. City of Talents? Berlin's Regional Economy, Socio-Spatial Fabric and "Worst Practice" Urban Governance. *International Journal of Urban and Regional Research* 28(3): 511–29; Beveridge, *A Politics of Inevitability*.

38 Fields, D. and Uffer, S. 2016. The Financialization of Rental Housing: A Comparative Analysis of New York City and Berlin. *Urban Studies* 53(7): 1486–1502.

39 Cf. Colomb, C. 2011. *Staging the New Berlin: Place Marketing and the Politics of Urban Reinvention post-1989*. London: Routledge; Bernt, M., Grell, B. and Holm, A. (eds.) 2013. *The Berlin Reader: A Compendium on Urban Change and Activism*. Bielefeld: transcript.

40 Holm, A. 2010. *Wir bleiben alle!: Gentrifizierung – städtische Konflikte um Aufwertung und Verdrängung*. Münster: Unrast.

41 Beveridge and Koch, Contesting Austerity, De-centring the State.
42 Mayer, First World Urban Activism; see also Briata, P., Colomb, C. and Mayer, M. 2020. Bridging across Difference in Contemporary (Urban) Social Movements: Territory as Catalyst. *Territory, Politics, Governance* 8(4): 451–60. And in the same issue: Hamann, U. and Türkmen, C. 2020. Communities of Struggle: The Making of a Protest Movement around Housing, Migration and Racism Beyond Identity Politics in Berlin. *Territory, Politics, Governance* 8(4): 515–31; Helbrecht, I. (ed.) 2016. *Gentrifizierung in Berlin: Verdrängungsprozesse und Bleibestrategien.* Bielefeld: transcript.
43 E.g. Davis, M. 1990. *City of Quartz: Excavating the Future of Los Angeles.* New York: Vintage Books; Keil, R. and Branfman, J. (eds.) 2019. *Public Los Angeles: A Private City's Activist Futures/Don Parson.* Athens: University of Georgia Press; Stepick, M.C. 2019. *Rebuilding Los Angeles: Labor-Community Coalition Organizing around Transit and Housing.* UCLA Dissertation in Sociology; Roy, A., Graziani, T. and Stephens, P. 2020. *Unhousing the Poor: Interlocking Regimes of Racialized Policing.* Paper for the Square One Project's Roundtable on Justice Policy, at https://challengeinequality.luskin.ucla.edu/2020/08/25/unhousing-the-poor.
44 Parson, D. 2005. *Making a Better World: Public Housing, the Red Scare, and the Direction of Modern Los Angeles.* Minneapolis: University of Minnesota Press: 7.
45 School of Echos. 2019. La COMUNA o NADA: Building an Autonomous Tenants Movement in Los Angeles. *dérive* 77: 19–26.
46 Rosenthal, T.J. 2016. 101 Notes on the LA Tenants Union (You Can't Do Politics Alone). In Roy, A. and Malson, H. (eds.). *Housing Justice in Unequal Cities*, at https://challengeinequality.luskin.ucla.edu/wp-content/uploads/sites/16/2019/10/Housing-Justice-in-Unequal-Cities.pdf.
47 School of Echos. La COMUNA o NADA: 26.
48 Roy, *Emergency Urbanism.*
49 Bhan et al., The Pandemic, Southern Urbanisms and Collective Life.

5 Urban Publics and Citizens

1 Nancy talks about this in terms of shared 'sense', see Nancy, J.-L. 2019. *Democracy and Community*. Cambridge: Polity: 92.
2 Boudreau, *Global Urban Politics*.
3 Cf. Carlsson, C. (ed.) 2002. *Critical Mass: Bicycling's Defiant Celebration*. San Francisco: AK Press. See also https://criticalmass.fandom.com/wiki/List_of_rides.
4 Holston, Metropolitan Rebellions and the Politics of Commoning the City.
5 Carlsson (ed.), *Critical Mass*.
6 Furness, Z. 2007. Critical Mass, Urban Space and Vélomobility. *Mobilities* 2(2): 300.
7 Strüver, A. 2015. Critical Mass als performative Kritik der städtischen Verkehrspolitik? Fahrradfahren mit Judith Butler auf dem Gepäckträger. *sub\urban* 3(3): 40.
8 Carlsson (ed.), *Critical Mass*: 81f.
9 Beveridge and Koch, Urban Everyday Politics; cf. Eckert, J. 2015. *Practice Movements: The Politics of Non-Sovereign Power*. In Della Porta, D. and Mario, D. (eds.) *The Oxford Handbook of Social Movements*. Oxford: Oxford University Press.
10 See also Thorpe, A. 2020. *Owning the Street: The Everyday Life of Property*. Cambridge, MA: MIT Press.
11 Parry, S. 2015. A Theatrical Gesture of Disavowal: The Civility of the Critical Mass Cycle Ride. *Contemporary Theatre Review* 25(3): 344–56. See also Flynn, A. 2016. Regulating Critical Mass: Performativity and City Streets. *Windsor Review of Legal and Social Issues* 37(1): 98–117.
12 Parry, A Theatrical Gesture of Disavowal: 351.
13 Ibid.
14 Ibid.: 354.
15 Furness, Critical Mass, Urban Space and Vélomobility.
16 Iveson, K. 2007. *Publics and the City*. Oxford: Blackwell: 8.
17 Cooper, D. 2016. Transformative State Publics. *New Political Science* 38(3): 315–34.
18 Ibid.
19 Mahoney, N. and Clarke, J. 2013. Public Crisis, Public Futures. *Cultural Studies* 27(6): 948.

20 Butler, Bodies in Alliance and the Politics of the Street.
21 Carlsson, C. 2011. King of the Road. *Boom: A Journal of California* 1(3), 80–7; but see also the political action by Ovarian Psycos: Hosek, J.R. 2017. Ovarian Psycos. *Transfers* 7(2): 120–3.
22 Vasudevan, *The Autonomous City*.
23 Yates, L. 2015. Everyday Politics, Social Practices and Movement Networks: Daily Life in Barcelona's Social Centres. *The British Journal of Sociology* 66(2): 236–58.
24 Garrett, B. 2013. *Explore Everything: Place-Hacking the City*. London: Verso.
25 Vinegar, R., Parker, P. and McCourt, G. 2016. More Than a Response to Food Insecurity: Demographics and Social Networks of Urban Dumpster Divers. *Local Environment* 21(2): 241–53.
26 Crossan, J., Cumbers, A., McMaster, R. and Shaw, D. 2016. Contesting Neoliberal Urbanism in Glasgow's Community Gardens: The Practice of DIY Citizenship. *Antipode* 48(4): 937–55.
27 Graham, J.K. 2008. Diverse Economies: Performative Practices for 'Other Worlds'. *Progress in Human Geography* 32(5): 613–32; Gritzas, G. and Kavoulakos, K.I. 2016. Diverse Economies and Alternative Spaces: An Overview of Approaches and Practices. *European Urban and Regional Studies* 23(4): 917–34; Calvo, S. and Morales, A. 2014. *Exploring Complementary Currencies in Europe: A Comparative Study of Local Initiatives in Spain and the United Kingdom*. London: Living in Minca.
28 Tummers, I.L. 2015. Introduction to the Special Issue: Towards a Long-Term Perspective of Self-Managed Collaborative Housing Initiatives. *Urban Research & Practice* 8(1): 1–4.
29 Vasudevan, *The Autonomous City*.
30 Parés, M., Boada, J., Canal, R., Hernando, E. and Martìnez, R. 2017. Challenging Collaborative Urban Governance under Austerity: How Local Governments and Social Organizations Deal with Housing Policy in Catalonia (Spain). *Journal of Urban Affairs* 39(8): 1066–84; Iveson, K. 2013. Cities Within the City: Do-It-Yourself Urbanism and

the Right to the City. *International Journal of Urban and Region Research* 37(3): 941–56.

31 Gilchrist, P. and Ravenscroft, N. 2013. Space Hijacking and the Anarcho-Politics of Leisure. *Leisure Studies* 32(1): 49–68.

32 Arampatzi, A. 2016. The Spatiality of Counter-Austerity Politics in Athens, Greece: Emergent Urban Solidarity Spaces. *Urban Studies* 54(9): 2155–71; Daskalaki, M. 2018. Alternative Organizing in Times of Crisis: Resistance Assemblages and Socio-Spatial Solidarity. *European Urban and Regional Studies* 25(2): 155–70; Stavrides, S. 2014. Emerging Common Spaces as a Challenge to the City of Crisis. *City* 18(4/5): 546–50; Kousis, M. and Paschou, M. 2017. Alternative Forms of Resilience: A Typology of Approaches for the Study of Citizen Collective Responses in Hard Economic Times. *Partecipazione & Conflitto* 10(1).

33 Hammelman, C. 2018. Urban Migrant Women's Everyday Food Insecurity Coping Strategies Foster Alternative Urban Imaginaries of a More Democratic Food System. *Urban Geography* 39(5): 706–25.

34 Ibid.: 711.

35 Ibid.: 713.

36 Ibid.: 715.

37 Ibid.: 710.

38 Arampatzi, A. 2017. Contentious Spatialities in an Era of Austerity: Everyday Politics and 'Struggle Communities' in Athens, Greece. *Political Geography* 60: 47–56.

39 Di Feliciantonio, C. 2017. Spaces of the Expelled as Spaces of the Urban Commons? Analysing the Re-emergence of Squatting Initiatives in Rome. *International Journal of Urban and Regional Research* 41: 708–25.

40 Arampatzi, Contentious Spatialities in an Era of Austerity.

41 Ibid.: 53.

42 Iveson, Cities Within the City.

43 Magnusson, *Politics of Urbanism*.

44 Isin, E.F. 2008. Theorizing Acts of Citizenship. In Isin, E.F. and Nielsen, G.M. (eds.) *Acts of Citizenship*. Basingstoke: Palgrave Macmillan: 15–43.

45 Isin, E.F. 2002. *Being Political: Genealogies of Citizenship*. Minneapolis: University of Minnesota Press.

46 Holston, Metropolitan Rebellions and the Politics of Commoning the City.
47 See e.g. Holston and Appadurai, Cities and Citizenship: 196.
48 Ibid.: 197.
49 Butcher, S. and Apsan F., A. 2014. Insurgent Citizenship Practices: The Case of Muungano wa Wanavijiji in Nairobi, Kenya. *City* 18(2): 119–33.
50 Holston, J. 2009. Insurgent Citizenship in an Era of Global Urban Peripheries. *Cities and Society* 21(2): 253–77.
51 McFarlane, C. and Silver, J. 2017. The Poolitical City: 'Seeing Sanitation' and Making the Urban Political in Cape Town. *Antipode* 49(1): 125–48.
52 Ibid.: 125.
53 Ibid.
54 Ibid.: 131.
55 Ibid.: 136.
56 Ibid.: 137.
57 Lemanski, C. 2020. Infrastructural Citizenship: The Everyday Citizenships of Adapting and/or Destroying Public Infrastructure in Cape Town, South Africa. *Transactions of the Institute of British Geographers* 45(3): 589–605.
58 Holston, Metropolitan Rebellions and the Politics of Commoning the City.
59 Ibid.: 123.
60 Ibid.: 128.
61 Ibid.: 121.
62 Ibid.: 121–2.
63 Roussos, K. 2019. Grassroots Collective Action within and beyond Institutional and State Solutions: The (Re-)politicization of Everyday Life in Crisis-Ridden Greece. *Social Movement Studies* 18(3): 265–83.
64 Kaika, M. and Karaliotas, L. 2016. The Spatialization of Democratic Politics: Insights from Indignant Squares. *European Urban and Regional Studies* 23(4): 566.
65 Ibid.
66 Boudreau, J-A., Boucher, N. and Liguori, M. 2009. Taking the Bus Daily and Demonstrating on Sunday: Reflections on the Formation of Political Subjectivity in an Urban World. *City* 13(2–3): 336–46.

67 Nicholls, W.J. and Uitermark, J. 2016. *Cities and Social Movements: Immigrant Rights Activism in the United States, France, and the Netherlands, 1970–2015*. Malden: Wiley Blackwell.
68 Ibid.: 227.
69 Ibid.
70 Minuchin, L., Maino, J., Bizzarri, M.J., Bertolaccini, L., Gomez, M.V. and Panero, C. 2020. Municipal Logistics: Popular Infrastructures and Southern Urbanisms During the Pandemic. Minim Report N.IV, at https://minim-municipalism.org/wp-content/uploads/2020/12/Municipal-logistics.pdf.
71 Ibid.: 4.
72 Ibid.
73 Ibid.: 3.
74 Minuchin et al. Municipal Logics: 3.
75 Boudreau, *Global Urban Politics*.
76 Ibid.
77 Hamilton, O.R. 2017. *The City Always Wins*. Faber: London.
78 Holston, Metropolitan Rebellions and the Politics of Commoning the City: 125; Featherstone, *Solidarity*.
79 Simone, A. 2004. People as Infrastructure: Intersecting Fragments in Johannesburg. *Public Culture* 16(3): 407.

6 Urban Democracy and the State

1 Boudreau, *Global Urban Politics*.
2 Kohn, Author Response; Cooper, Transformative State Publics.
3 Allen, J. and Cochrane, A. 2010. Assemblages of State Power: Topological Shifts in the Organization of Government and Politics. *Antipode* 42(5): 1071–89.
4 Russell, Beyond the Local Trap; Cooper, D. 2017. Prefiguring the State. *Antipode* 49(2): 335–56.
5 Thompson, What's New about New Municipalism?
6 Baiocchi, *We, the Sovereign*: ix.
7 The new urban left of the 1980s in the UK might also be seen in these terms. See Martin, B. and Fudge, C. 1984. *Local Socialism*. London: Macmillan.

8 Baiocchi, G. and Gies, H. 2019. Radical Cities in Latin America: Past and Present. *NACLA Report on the Americas* 51(4): 313.
9 Ibid.: 314.
10 E.g. Barcelona en Comú activist Kate Shea Baird, quoted in Angel, J. 2021. New Municipalism and the State: Remunicipalising Energy in Barcelona, from Prosaics to Process. *Antipode* 53(2): 526.
11 Brown, *Undoing the Demos*.
12 Kohn, *Urban Commonwealth*: 159ff.
13 Cooper, Prefiguring the State.
14 On the local state, see Cochrane, A. 2016. Thinking about the 'Local' of Local Government: A Brief History of Invention and Reinvention. *Local Government Studies* 42 (6): 907–15.
15 London Edinburgh Weekend Return Group. 1980. *In and Against the State*. London: Pluto. Cf. Cumbers, A. 2015. Constructing a Global Commons in, against and beyond the State. *Space and Polity* 19(1): 62–75.
16 Cf. Baiocchi, *We, the Sovereign*: 84.
17 Cooper, Transformative State Publics; and Cooper, Prefiguring the State.
18 Cooper, Transformative State Publics: 316.
19 Cooper, D. 1993. An Engaged State: Sexuality, Governance, and the Potential for Change. *Journal of Law and Society* 20(3): 257.
20 Cooper, Transformative State Publics: 316.
21 Cooper, D. 2019. *Feeling Like a State*. Durham, NC: Duke University Press: 173.
22 Cooper, Prefiguring the State: 338.
23 Aretxaga B. 2003. Maddening States. *Annual Review of Anthropology* 32(1): 393–410; and Scott, J. 2009. *The Art of Not Being Governed*. New Haven: Yale University Press, cited in Cooper, Prefiguring the State: 338.
24 Hanna, T.M., Guinan, J. and Bilsborough, J. 2018. *The 'Preston Model' and the Modern Politics of Municipal Socialism*. At https://neweconomics.opendemocracy.net/preston-model-modern-politics-municipal-socialism.
25 Ibid.: 2.
26 CLES and Preston City Council. 2018. How We Built Community Wealth in Preston. At https://www.preston.

gov.uk/media/1792/How-we-built-community-wealth-in-Preston/pdf/CLES_Preston_Document_WEB_AW.pdf?m=636994067328930000.

27 Ibid.: 2.

28 Hastings, A., Bailey, N., Bramley, G. and Gannon, M. 2017. Austerity Urbanism in England: The 'Regressive Redistribution' of Local Government Services and the Impact on the Poor and Marginalised. *Environment and Planning A: Economy and Space* 49(9): 2007–24.

29 Thompson, M. 2021. The Uses and Abuses of Municipalism on the British Left. *Minim*, 13 April, at https://minim-municipalism.org/magazine/the-uses-and-abuses-of-municipalism-by-the-british-left.

30 Brown, M. and Jones, R.E. 2021. *Paint Your Town Red*. London: Repeater Books: 134.

31 Boddy and Fudge (eds.), *Local Socialism*.

32 Thompson, What's New about New Municipalism?

33 Cooperation Jackson, Who We Are. At https://cooperationjackson.org/intro.

34 Forster, M.D. and Rehner, T. 2018. Prospects for Progressive Politics in Mississippi. *Race, Gender & Class* 25(2/3): 124.

35 See Akuno, K. 2017. Build and Fight: The Program and Strategy of Cooperation Jackson. In *Jackson Rising*, at https://jacksonrising.pressbooks.com/chapter/build-and-fight-the-program-and-strategy-of-cooperation-jackson.

36 ROAR collective. Dual Power Then and Now: From the Iroquois to Cooperation Jackson. At https://roarmag.org/magazine/dual-power-then-and-now-from-the-iroquois-to-cooperation-jackson.

37 See Lumumba, R. 2017. Foreword to *Jackson Rising*. At https://jacksonrising.pressbooks.com/front-matter/realizing-self-determination.

38 See https://cooperationjackson.org/lumumba-center.

39 Blanco et al., Urban Governance and Political Change; Russell, Beyond the Local Trap; Thompson, What's New about New Municipalism?

40 Russell, Beyond the Local Trap: 1002.

41 Thompson, What's New about New Municipalism?: 321.

42 Angel, New Municipalism and the State: 526.

43 Beveridge and Featherstone, Introduction: Anti-Politics, Austerity and Spaces of Politicisation: 445.
44 Davies, *Between Realism and Revolt.*
45 Thompson, What's New about New Municipalism?: 326.
46 Pill, M. 2021. *Governing Cities*. Cham: Palgrave Macmillan: 135.
47 Ibid.
48 Della Porta, D., Fernández, J., Kouki, H. and Mosca, L. 2017. *Movement Parties Against Austerity*. Cambridge: Polity.
49 Zechner, M. 2015. Barcelona en Comú: The City as Horizon for Democracy. *Roar Magazine*, 4 March, at https://roarmag.org/essays/barcelona-en-Comú-guanyem.
50 Angel, New Municipalism and the State: 525.
51 Russell, Beyond the Local Trap: 998.
52 Pinto, M., Recano, L. and Rossi, U. 2022. New Institutions and the Politics of the Interstices: Experimenting With a Face-to-Face Democracy in Naples. *Urban Studies*, DOI: 10.1177/00420980221091064.
53 De Majo, E. 2020. Neomunicipalism in Naples. *Minim*, 17 March, at https://minim-municipalism.org/magazine/neomunicipalism-in-naples.
54 Ibid.
55 Pinto, Recano and Rossi, New Institutions.
56 Russell, Beyond the Local Trap: 998.
57 Pinto, Recano and Rossi, New Institutions: 3.
58 Ibid.: 11.
59 Keane, J. 2009. Monitory Democracy and Media-Saturated Societies. *Griffith Review* 24: 47–69.
60 Beveridge, R. and Naumann, M. 2021. Progressive Urbanism in Small Towns: The Contingencies of Governing from the Left. *Urban Affairs Review*. DOI: https://doi.org/10.1177/10780874211055834.

7 The City in the Age of Urbanization

1 Brown, W. 2019. *In the Ruins of Neoliberalism: The Rise of the Antidemocratic Politics in the West.* New York: Columbia University Press; Crouch, *Post-Democracy*; Streeck, *How Will Capitalism End?*

2 Lees, L., Shin, H.B. and López-Morales, E. 2016. *Planetary Gentrification*. Cambridge: Polity.
3 Atkinson, *Alpha City*.
4 Smith, D. 1994. *Geography and Social Justice*. Oxford: Blackwell.
5 Slater, T. 2021. *Shaking up the City: Ignorance, Inequality and the Urban Question*. Berkeley: University of California Press.
6 Isin, City.State: Critique of Scalar Thought.
7 See https://tfn.scot/news/campaigners-warn-home-office-you-messed-with-the-wrong-city.
8 See https://www.independent.co.uk/news/uk/home-news/glasgow-protests-refugee-far-right-arrests-police-a9571941.html.
9 See https://tfn.scot/news/campaigners-warn-home-office-you-messed-with-the-wrong-city.
10 Massey, D. 2005. *For Space*. London: Sage.
11 *May Day Manifesto 1967–68*. A re-issue of the text of the May Day Manifesto, at https://lwbooks.co.uk/wp-content/uploads/woocommerce_uploads/2021/03/Mayday-Manifesto-0mkcyo.pdf.
12 Wolin, *Fugitive Democracy*: 100.
13 See https://www.die-urbane.de.
14 Held, D. 1997. *Democracy and the Global Order: From the Modern State to Cosmopolitan Governance*. Cambridge: Polity.
15 Wolin, *Fugitive Democracy*.
16 Ibid.: 54.
17 Keil, The Empty Shell of the Planetary.
18 Barnett, What Do Cities Have to Do with Democracy?
19 Simone and Pieterse, *New Urban Worlds*.
20 Beveridge and Koch, Urban Everyday Politics; Iveson, Cities Within the City.
21 Boudreau, *Global Urban Politics*.
22 Beveridge and Koch, Urban Everyday Politics.
23 Fraser, N. 2016. Expropriation and Exploitation in Racialized Capitalism: A Reply to Michael Dawson. *Critical Historical Studies* 3(1): 163–78.
24 Kohn, *Urban Commonwealth*.
25 Young, *Justice and the Politics of Difference*: 237.

26 Massey, D. 1994. *Space, Place and Gender*. Minneapolis: University of Minnesota Press.
27 Blokland, T. 2017. *Community as Practice*. Cambridge: Polity.
28 Clarke, N., Jennings, W., Moss, J. and Stoker, G. 2018. *The Good Politician: Folk Theories, Political Interaction, and the Rise of Anti-Politics*. Cambridge: Cambridge University Press.

Index

Index

Index

Index

Index

Index

Index

Index